"Zhongxian Wu and Karin Taylor Wu have accomplished the feat of producing a readable account of GanZhi, one of the most complex subjects among the gnostic sciences of ancient China: the detailed calculation of how, exactly, the Above and the Below interweave and create qualitative differences in our space-time environment. A must read for every serious student of classical Chinese medicine and ancient cosmology."

—*Heiner Fruehauf, Ph.D., Founding Professor, School of Classical Chinese Medicine, National College of Natural Medicine*

"From, to, and for the Great Oneness comes a soul size gift in the form of a book—*Heavenly Stems and Earthly Branches*—given to all of us to help us live, to help us stay awake to the heartbeat of being and to help us to help others know themselves as the pulse of goodness and beauty between heaven and earth. I thank you, wonderful couple Master and Dr. Taylor Wu, on behalf of all of us. I bow to you in gratitude."

—*Dianne M. Connelly, Ph.D., M.Ac. (UK), co-founder of Tai Sophia Institute (now known as Maryland University of Integrative Health), author, and Chinese medicine practitioner*

"This beautiful and timely book re-establishes Heavenly Stems and Earthly Branches as a central tenet of Chinese philosophy and an intimate part of Chinese medicine, not an optional extra. Liberally illustrated with diagrams and backed by classical quotations, quietly authoritative writers Zhongxian Wu and Karin Taylor Wu share their deep knowledge to produce a kaleidoscopic presentation, bridging the ancient Chinese traditions of medicine, Yin Yang Five Phase theory, Yijing studies, cosmology, music, and internal alchemy. From star pattern etymology for Chinese characters to practical seasonal advice, from discussion of the application of hidden stems to the complexities of alchemical transformation, this book serves as an essential primer that will be of use to beginner and advanced practitioner alike in the study of the pulsing rhythms of unfolding time."

—*Peter Firebrace, Past Principal of the International College of Oriental Medicine, co-founder of Monkey Press, acupuncturist, author, and teacher*

"This is an excellent portrayal of the philosophy of the Stems and Branches—TianGan DiZhi! It brings a fuller context to the subject for experienced practitioners by investigating each of the 22 characters of the GanZhi through calligraphy, poems from various sources in Chinese literature, and cultural artefacts. It also introduces those new to this area of Chinese culture and medicine to exciting concepts that will help to take clinical practice to another dimension."

—*Sam Patel, Joint Principal, The International College of Oriental Medicine*

"The subject of Stems and Branches is a real challenge for everyone who studies or works in the field of classical Chinese medicine. This wonderful book, based on authentic classical texts, is of great importance for those who seek deeper understanding for the sake of the health and peace of their patients and themselves. I am grateful to Master Wu and Dr. Karin Taylor Wu for their inspiration and for opening gateways into the hidden knowledge of the fundamentals of Chinese Medicine."

—*Joan Duveen, M.Ac., practitioner and teacher of acupuncture according to the Heavenly Stems and Earthly Branches*

"Master Wu and Dr. Taylor Wu's outstanding new book introduces the basic principles, key applications, imagery, poetry and philosophy of the ancient science of TianGan DiZhi. The study of 'Heavenly Stems and Earthly Branches' is an important gateway opening to a deeper understanding of applied Chinese Philosophy, and especially the inner aspects of Traditional Medicine, Geomancy, Pugilism, Music Theory and Taoist Internal Alchemy. Written with a distinctive flair for Chinese scholarship, this book cuts deep into the heart of the matter. If you strive to achieve a better understanding of your Chinese art, this book will certainly guide you towards the correct path."

—*Ioannis Solos, Chinese medicine practitioner, researcher and author, Beijing, China*

Heavenly Stems and Earthly Branches
TianGan DiZhi

by the same authors

Companion Study Card Set
Heavenly Stems and Earthly Branches—TianGan DiZhi
The Keys to the Sublime
Master Zhongxian Wu and Dr. Karin Taylor Wu
ISBN 978 1 84819 150 1

The 12 Chinese Animals
Create Harmony in your Daily Life through Ancient Chinese Wisdom
Master Zhongxian Wu
ISBN 978 1 84819 031 3
eISBN 978 0 85701 015 5

XinYi WuDao
Heart-Mind—The Dao of Martial Arts
Master Zhongxian Wu
ISBN 978 1 84819 206 5
eISBN 978 0 85701 156 5

Fire Dragon Meridian Qigong
Essential NeiGong for Health and Spiritual Transformation
Master Zhongxian Wu and Dr. Karin Taylor Wu
ISBN 978 1 84819 103 7
eISBN 978 0 85701 085 8

Chinese Shamanic Cosmic Orbit Qigong
Esoteric Talismans, Mantras, and Mudras in Healing and Inner Cultivation
Master Zhongxian Wu
ISBN 978 1 84819 056 6
eISBN 978 0 85701 059 9

Seeking the Spirit of The Book of Change
8 Days to Mastering a Shamanic Yijing (I Ching) Prediction System
Master Zhongxian Wu
Foreword by Daniel Reid
ISBN 978 1 84819 020 7
eISBN 978 0 85701 007 0

Vital Breath of the Dao
Chinese Shamanic Tiger Qigong—Laohu Gong
Master Zhongxian Wu
Foreword by Chungliang Al Huang
ISBN 978 1 84819 000 9
eISBN 978 0 85701 110 7

Heavenly Stems and Earthly Branches
TianGan DiZhi

The Heart of Chinese Wisdom Traditions

Master Zhongxian Wu and Dr. Karin Taylor Wu

Foreword by Fei BingXun

SINGING
DRAGON

LONDON AND PHILADELPHIA

First published in hardback in 2014
Paperback edition first published in 2016
by Singing Dragon
an imprint of Jessica Kingsley Publishers
73 Collier Street
London N1 9BE, UK
and
400 Market Street, Suite 400
Philadelphia, PA 19106, USA

www.singingdragon.com

Library of Congress Cataloging in Publication Data
A CIP catalog record for this book is available from the Library of Congress

British Library Cataloguing in Publication Data
A CIP catalogue record for this book is available from the British Library

ISBN 978 1 84819 208 9
eISBN 978 0 85701 158 9

Printed and bound in China

This book is dedicated to

Wu WenPu 吳文甫 *and Guo JinYu* 郭金玉
Peyton Troy Taylor and Helena Ström Taylor
Li MingZhong 李明忠 *and Hua AnMei* 華安梅

千總之行隨明法

以方三才藏玄機

天顛夢枕連容編

仁海書

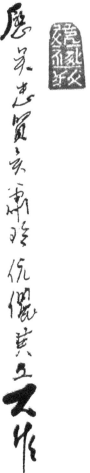

天圆一气顯其道

願吳忠賢吳簫玲伉儷英文大作

天干地支真道密鑰在傅布道家易醫

丹功造福全球作出貢獻興旺發達

天圓一氣顯真道

干總五行隱明德

地方三才藏玄機

支類萬物透密鑰

癸巳孟春

任法融

With permission, we have transcribed Grandmaster Ren's elegant calligraphy blessings into Chinese type font (above) and translated his words into English (next page).

Blessings from Daoist Grandmaster
Ren FaRong 任法融

YuanWuZhongxianWuXiaolingHangLiYingWenDaZuo
TianGanDiZhiZhenDaoMiYueZaiChuanBuDaoJiaYiYiDanGong
ZaoFuQuanQiuZuoChuGongXianXingWanFaDa

TianYuanYiQiXianZhenDao
GanZongWuXingYinMingDe

DiFangSanCaiCangXuanJi
ZhiLeiWanWuTouMiYue

Blessings to the couple Wu Zhongxian and Wu Xiaoling for their extraordinary work: *Heavenly Stems and Earthly Branches: The Heart of Chinese Wisdom Traditions.* This book offers an unprecedented contribution to Daoism, the Yijing, traditional medicine, internal alchemy and Qigong practice to the English-speaking world. My wish is for this offering to bring great benefits to people throughout the world. May it flourish and prosper!

The Heavenly Way circles with One-Qi,
showing the truth of the Dao
Stems rule the Five Elements, the hidden way of Enlightenment

The Earthly Way secures the Trinity, storing the mystical trigger
Branches symbolize Ten-Thousand-Things
and reveal the keys to the sublime

Grandmaster Ren FaRong, former abbot of LouGuanTai 樓觀台 *(where LaoZi wrote his DaoDeJing) is China's leading scholar of the DaoDeJing, the Yijing and Daoist internal alchemy practices and has published numerous books in this field. Grandmaster Ren currently serves as president of ZhongGuoDaoJiaoXieHui* 中國道教協會 *(Chinese Daoist Association).*

The authors received Grandmaster Ren's blessings for this work at LouGuanTai in February 2013

Authors' Notes

- We have chosen to capitalize all Chinese *PinYin* words and phrases throughout this book. On first introduction, each will appear translated alongside the appropriate Chinese characters.

- All Chinese *PinYin* words and phrases will be italicized with the exception of the ten Heavenly Stem names and twelve Earthly Branch names as well as widely used Chinese words, for example, Dao, Yin, Yang, Qigong, Taiji, etc.

- When the following words are capitalized—Five Elements, Element, Water, Wood, Fire, Earth, and Metal—they refer specifically to the Chinese *WuXing* 五行 (Five Elements). When you see Heavenly Stems, Earthly Branches, Stem(s), and Branch(es) capitalized, we are referring specifically to the Chinese GanZhi 干支 (Heavenly Stems and Earthly Branches).

- Passages of Chinese logograms are presented in the traditional style and read from top to bottom, right to left. Modern *PinYin* reads conventionally, left to right.

- As the GanZhi were developed in the northern hemisphere, any seasonal and directional related terms in this book refer to those in the northern hemisphere.

Contents

List of Figures and Tables

Figures

Tables

Acknowledgments

This book bears the fruit of many years of the teaching and consultations we have offered, both as individual practitioners and together as a family. With clasped hands, we extend our heartfelt appreciation for our students and our clients, whose enthusiasm for pursuing the roots of ancient Chinese wisdom has encouraged us to continue sharing the GanZhi with others.

Ten thousand thank-yous to all our Qi friends who have provided their support during this project—most particularly, Daoist Grandmaster Ren FaRong 任法融, Master Ren XingZhi 任興之 (the abbot of Daoist ancestral temple *LouGuanTai*), and Professor Fei BingXun 費秉勛.

To Jessica Kingsley and her Singing Dragon, for her excitement about this book as she patiently watched us draw it into life—we are grateful for our shared *YuanFen* 緣份!

Our deepest gratitude is bestowed upon our teachers, masters, and families, with a special mention to Master Li MingZhong 李明忠 for his beautiful "Rhythm of Qi" calligraphy and a lifetime of guidance.

的規律，與宇宙運行相應，天干、地支的自然背景也在天文。所以中國文化最厚實的背景是天文，天干、地支建立人類生產生活的准則。

西漢是中國易學的白銀時代，其中以孟喜、京房為代表的象數易派，數千年的易學成果，把八卦、陰陽、五行、四時、日月運行、干支等組建為一個有機的系統，他們以天干地支為時間空間軸創立卦氣、納甲、飛伏、世應的象數模式，明白了代表事物的天干地支，因此，歸屬、性質及其所處環境的聯繫，就容易把握該事物的處境。

哲學家馮友蘭說易學就是「宇宙代數學」，要認識事物，就把相關的元數（包括干支）代入其中，即可推求事物的一切情況。望《天干地支》一書能幫你掌握干支密碼，從而去解開生命與宇宙天干地支之真相。

*費秉勳繫中國易學院院長，西北大學文學院教授，著有《八卦占卜新解》和《奇門遁甲新述》等十多部書。

天干地支在易學文化中的作用和地位

費秉勛 *

在中國易學文化中，天干地支是事物所處時空座標和事物性質的宇宙秘碼。

傳說在四千七百多年前的黃帝時代，黃帝之臣大撓創制了天干地支而根據可靠的文字（甲骨文）資料，天干地支在夏商時代中華先民就起碼在商時代就用天干地支用。中國史書《春秋公羊傳》明確記載：魯隱公三年這里的己巳就是用天干地支紀日，魯隱公三年是公元前七二零年，三年春西一年二月己巳日，己巳日發生了日食之"。這里的己巳就是用天干地支紀日。越西漢以后則通用干支紀年紀時。隨着歷史的發展，天干地支越來越向中國文化滲透，其內涵也越來越深邃豐富。

中國文化"天人合一"特征的一個重要方面就是"法天"。先賢們從對日月星辰運行和大地萬物生長衰亡的觀察體證中，認識宇宙運動

The Role of TianGan DiZhi
in Yijng (I Ching) Culture

Fei BingXun 費秉勛

In Chinese Yijing culture, TianGan DiZhi, the Heavenly Stems and Earthly Branches, define the time-space axis of the universe and unlock the nature of everything in existence. They are the secret code of the universal way.

According to legend, it was during the period of the Yellow Emperor [about 4700 years ago], that DaRao 大撓, minister of the Yellow Emperor, created the codifying symbols of TianGan DiZhi. Historical written documents (oracle bones) dating back at least as far as the Xia and Shang dynasties [2070–1600 BCE and 1600–1046 BCE, respectively] reveal ancient Chinese used these GanZhi symbols in a calendrical system to mark each day. The Chinese history book, *ChunQiu GongYangZhuan* 春秋公羊傳 [GongYang's Commentary on the Spring and Autumn Annals], clearly documents this: "In February, the spring of LuYinGong 魯隱公's third year, during the day of JiSi 己巳, there was an eclipse." LuYinGong's third year was 720 BCE, and the use of JiSi in this text shows us that the GanZhi symbols have been used to chronicle time and events for over 2700 years. The GanZhi have been used continuously in the official records of the Chinese calendrical system since the Western Han Dynasty [1046–771 BCE]. As history has developed, the GanZhi system has penetrated all aspects of Chinese culture, carrying deeper and richer meaning with time.

TianRenHeYi 天人合一—"human beings follow the way of Heaven"—is a central tenet of Chinese tradition. By observing the unbroken revolution of the sun, moon, and stars in the sky and nature's pattern of growth and decline on the earth, Chinese sages learned the laws of the universe and established their lives and living standards in accordance with the universal way. All traditional Chinese culture formed its roots in astronomy and the GanZhi formed its roots in the same cosmic soil. The Western Han Dynasty is known as the Silver Age of Chinese Yijing history, during which time Yijing masters Meng Xi 孟喜 and Jing Fang 京房

brought the renowned *XiangShu* 象數 [symbolism and numerology] Yijing school to the forefront of Yijing history. Through exhaustive study of astronomy and integration of thousands of years of Yijing study, these masters were able to organize the Bagua, YinYang, Yijing numerology, the movements of sun and moon, GanZhi, Five Elements, four seasons, and more into an organic system of living knowledge, creating the entire *XiangShu* system, including [but not limited to] *GuaQi* 卦氣 [the quality of Qi of each hexagram]; *NaJia* 納甲 [installing the GanZhi to each line of the hexagram]; *FeiFu* 飛伏 [Flying and Hidden divination method], and *ShiYing* 世應 [Self and Other relationships]. Within the *XiangShu* system, the GanZhi represent the YinYang and Five Element aspects of the time–space axis, allowing the mystic to explore and understand the character and nature of all things. Feng Youlan 馮友蘭, a highly regarded Chinese philosopher and Yijing scholar, is known to have said that the Yijing contains an incipient "algebra of the universe"—by plugging in the GanZhi, we can access a way to solve all Mystery. I hope this book, *Heavenly Stems and Earthly Branches—TianGan DiZhi: The Heart of Chinese Wisdom Traditions*, will help you master the secrets of the GanZhi and unravel the truth of life and of the universe itself.

Professor Fei BingXun is the president of ZhongGou YiXueYuan 中國易學院 *(Chinese Yijing College) and professor of XiBei DaXue* 西北大學 *(Northwest University), both located in Xi'an, China. He has authored over ten books on Yijing divination and classical Chinese literature.*

RenTianZhiDao 人天之道

The Way of Man and Nature

"The Way of Man and Nature"
Unless otherwise noted, all of the calligraphy in this book was created by Master Zhongxian Wu.

Since 2005, I have been writing quarterly newsletters to support subscribers on this path of Daoist inner cultivation and peaceful living. In each newsletter, I provide cosmological forecasts that describe upcoming changes in weather patterns, their effects on our health, and basic guidance on relevant cultivation practices. I base my predictions on the ancient system of Chinese cosmology that is richly preserved in the *HuangDiNeiJing* 黃帝內經 (*Yellow Emperor's Inner Canon*—the doctrinal source for Chinese medicine for the last two thousand years). At the heart of this system lies TianGan DiZhi 天干地支.

I would like to give you some examples of putting your knowledge of TianGan DiZhi (commonly abbreviated to GanZhi) to good use. On January 16, 2008, while I was still living in Portland, Oregon, I made the following prediction in my Year of Rat greetings letter:

> The spring of *WuZi* 戊子, the **Year of Earth Rat**, will start on February 4, 2008, although the Chinese New Year will be February 7, 2008 according to Chinese Cosmology. Actually, we can feel the spring energy now even in the Pacific Northwest. I walked outside earlier today and was surprised that the sprouts of the spring flowers were standing several inches out of the ground already and it seems that they are ready to bloom. **But this does not mean that it will be warm all the time after February 4, 2008. We might have a spring snowstorm in late March or early April**...

In late March and early April of 2008, I received many emails from friends expressing their surprise at how accurate the Chinese cosmological system was. On March 28, 2008, local Portland television station KATU reported: "An unusual late-season push of cold winter air into the Northwest brought snow to many locations...the snow event was recorded as the latest seasonal snowfall ever recorded [in the Portland area]. The previous record was March 10, set in 1951."[1]

In a more recent example, on May 3, 2013, I wrote the following in my 2013 summer greetings:

> Although we are still experiencing chilly nights and some cool days, the summer season will begin this year at 16:18 on May 5, 2013. *TaiYang HanShui* 太陽寒水 (Cold Water) energy will continue until **May 20th when *JueYin FengMu* 厥陰風木 (Wind Wood) energy takes over. Likely, this summer will have more powerful windstorms** than the last few summers...

---

1   www.katu.com/news/17082391.html

On the afternoon of Monday, May 20, 2013, an EF5 tornado, with peak winds estimated at 210 miles per hour (340 km/h), struck an Oklahoma City suburb (Moore, Oklahoma), tragically destroying over 10,000 homes, killing 24 people (including 10 children), injuring 377 others, and causing an estimated $2 billion in damage.[1]

Thousands of years ago, ancient Chinese sages used this system to accurately forecast national weather patterns, much like the experts of modern day NOAA (the US National Oceanic and Atmospheric Administration) do for us today. In Chapter 71 of the *HuangDiNeiJing*, we are told:

$$
\begin{matrix}
\cdots & 上 & 癸 \\
災 & 厥 & 巳 \\
九 & 陰 & \cdots \\
宮 & 木 & \\
\cdots & \cdots &
\end{matrix}
$$

GuiSi … ShangJueYinMu … ZaiJiuGong

The Year of GuiSi [GuiSi recurs every 60 years, most recently February 4, 2013–February 4, 2014]…the first half of the year will be dominated by *JueYin* Wood [Wind Energy]…and disasters will frequently appear in the 9th Palace [i.e. the south central location of a nation].

Accordingly, I was not surprised to learn about the terrible tornado in Oklahoma on May 20, or that "super-tornados" and other major natural disasters continued to occur throughout the summer of 2013 in the south central area of many countries. Using the guidance of the *HuangDiNeiJing*, we can learn to predict and prepare for natural disasters on a global scale and also how to predict and prepare for how the universal energy will affect us as individuals. For example, under these same conditions, I expect emergency rooms across the globe to see an increase in stroke and heart attack victims and for Chinese medicine practitioners to see an influx of patients suffering from wind invasion, heart problems and digestive disturbances. The ancient knowledge of the Heavenly Stems and Earthly Branches is timeless.

The 22 symbols that make up GanZhi hold the keys to the crucial alchemical principles that allow us to access the harmonious path of the Dao. The Daoist ideal holds that we strive to understand the patterns of nature and to cultivate daily practices that then allow us to live in harmony with our

---

1   http://en.wikipedia.org/wiki/2013_Moore_tornado

families and within our communities, extending to include harmonious co-existence with all the beings that share life on this planet and with the natural world.

The Heavenly Stems and Earthly Branches play a fundamental role in all classical Chinese traditions: Chinese astrology (the principle of your destiny), Chinese cosmology ("As above, so below," or the macrocosm and microcosm), FengShui 風水 (optimizing your life), Yijing 易經 (the way of choice), classical Chinese medicine (the art of health), classical Chinese music (the resonance of harmonious sounds), traditional Chinese calligraphy (painting with the breath), and Daoist internal alchemy (the art of immortality).

Regarding Daoist internal alchemy, many classical Qigong practices involve using the Stems and Branches as special tools to refine the Qi of our five organs systems and twelve meridians. For example, the diagram on the following page is from the well-known Daoist internal alchemy book *XingMingGuiZhi* 性命圭旨, which was first printed in 1615 CE. It shows the Heavenly Stems written inside their related organs. To the right, the Earthly Branches are used in an extensive description of the timing and the path of *Yuan* Qi 元氣 (original Qi) as it moves through various spiritual points in the body.

With proper guidance of GanZhi, one will be able to live a healthier and more peaceful existence by transforming large obstacles into smaller ones and by transforming small obstacles into no obstacle at all. For example, since the 1980s I have been using my study of *BaZi MingLi* 八字命理—Chinese astrology—to help thousands of people optimize their karma and experience of life. Each individual's astrological chart is constructed around eight GanZhi symbols and is a life reading that provides insight into a person's past, present, and future. By understanding the energy of the macrocosmic Universe at the moment of birth, we can understand how to best support the life patterns of the individual. Many people value the guidance a good *BaZhi* reading can provide around finding a new job, relocating to a new city, creating a plan for a promising business venture, finding an auspicious day for closing a deal, selecting favorable travel days, improving health and the quality of life, and choosing a harmonious wedding day, etc.

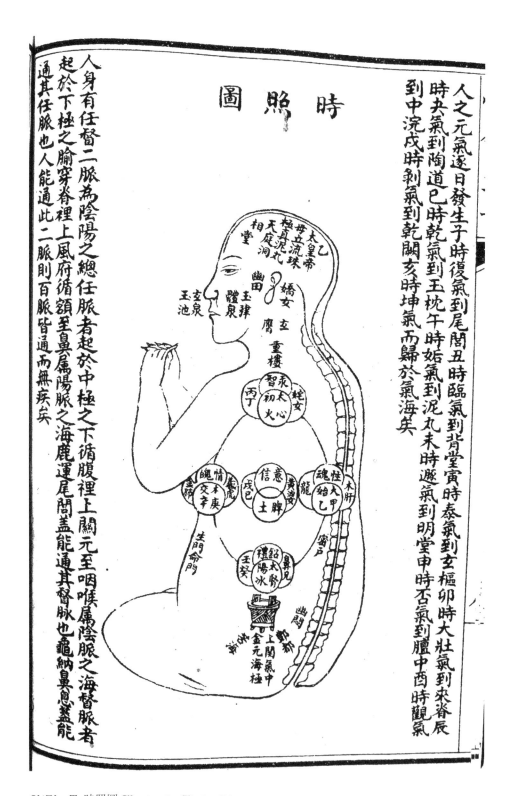

圖 照 時

人之元氣逐日發生子時復氣到尾閭丑時臨氣到背堂寅時
時夬氣到陶道巳時乾氣到玉枕午時姤氣到泥丸未時遯氣
到中浣戌時剝氣到乾關亥時坤氣而歸於氣海矣

人身有任督二脈為陰陽之總任脈者起於中極之下循腹裡上關元至咽喉屬陰脈之海督脈者
起於下極之腧穿脊裡上風府循額至鼻屬陽脈之海鹿運尾閭蓋能通其督脈也龜納鼻息盍能
通其任脈也人能通此二脈則百脈皆通而無疾矣

ShiZhaoTu 時照圖 *Illumination Timing Diagram*

In my hometown, like most rural towns throughout China, there has been a strong culture around arranged marriages. Judging from my own direct observation and my interviews with elders in my hometown, before the 1980s most people had no chance to speak with his or her future spouse until well after the marriage ceremony took place. This was true of my parents and my brother and sister-in-law. Before making a marriage arrangement for their children, all parents would hire an expert to check the compatibility of the birth charts of the potential couple. If it was determined that the two charts were well-matched, the parents proceeded with the marriage negotiations. If the two charts did not complement one another, the proposed arrangement would stop. I have observed that most of these arranged couples have stable and happy marriages. My parents enjoyed their 50 years together until my father recently passed away.

In the late 1980s, as China opened up to Western influence, free dating and free choice marriages quickly took over our old-fashioned traditions. Divorce rates in China increased exponentially. Today, many young people are returning to tradition, making sure they have an astrology consultation before committing their lives to one another. In modern China, GanZhi experts are sought out to provide astrology consultations concerning everything from potential marriages, business deals, health issues and real estate matters to funeral dates and more, and are still a vital part of daily life in my hometown and all over China. Even since leaving China in 2001, many of my Chinese friends and students still consult with me for GanZhi readings when at a crossroads or facing some challenges in their lives.

Our book, *The 12 Chinese Animals: Create Harmony in your Daily Life through Ancient Chinese Wisdom* (published by Singing Dragon in 2010), sheds light on the rich symbolic meanings of twelve animals of the Chinese zodiac as well their relationship to the Yijing, Chinese cosmology, astrology, and Daoist internal cultivation practices. Since its publication, many friends have expressed interest in learning more about how the GanZhi relate to the ancient science of Chinese cosmology and astrology. The twelve Chinese animals serve as physical representations of the Earthly Branches. In this book, we discuss the historical and mythological background of the twelve Earthly Branches and their ten Heavenly Stem companions to crystalize the symbolic meanings and the Five Elements alchemical transformation principles of the GanZhi.

It might be difficult to learn Chinese wisdom arts if you are trying to understand it from a logical, purely analytic mindset. For instance, Chinese medicine is *ZangXiang* 臟象 (Organ Symbol) medicine, which was established by Yijing *XiangShu* 象數—symbolism and numerology. In Chinese medicine, when an organ is referenced, it is not referenced as merely a physical organ; it is a symbol of the organic organ system itself as well as any part of the body that has a deep physical or energetic connection to it. In this book, we focus on decoding important *XiangShu* messages from the 22 GanZhi symbols, which themselves serve as the building blocks of all ancient Chinese wisdom traditions. We have also included simple GanZhi internal alchemy practices to help you gain bodily experience of the GanZhi *XiangShu*.

When I was working directly with Chinese medicine students, it usually took them two to three years of studying the symbolic meanings of the GanZhi before they were ready to apply their knowledge to Chinese cosmology, classical Chinese medicine, astrology, FengShui, *ZhiWuLiuZhu* 子午流注 (Optimizing Five Phases Acupuncture), their cultivation practice, and the Yijing prediction and diagnosis systems. Please be aware that this book is not an instructional text about Chinese astrology or other traditional arts. Like a specialty warehouse that carries the high-quality fundamental components needed to construct a home that will stand for generations, this book provides you with excellent information that will allow you to develop a solid foundation in GanZhi *XiangShu*. Please remember that getting the supplies is a preliminary step. Using this knowledge as you develop your skillset and grow into mastery (whether it be of the classical Chinese arts, Chinese classical texts, Chinese medicine, or as a Daoist practitioner) requires the guidance of an experienced teacher. For those who are already proficient, we hope our treasure trove of building materials in this spiritual warehouse will help you refine your expertise.

From our teaching experience we have found that many students and practitioners, especially during their first years of study, find it challenging to remember all of the symbols and the meanings of the GanZhi. With this in mind, we designed a companion study card set, *Heavenly Stems and Earthly Branches— TianGan DiZhi: The Keys to the Sublime*, modelled after Karin's personal study materials, to create a useful clinical and study tool for students of all Chinese wisdom traditions. The cards also show the correct stroke order for each

GanZhi character, for, as we say in China, *YanGuoShiBianBuRuShouGuoYiBian* 眼過十遍不如手過一遍—reading ten times is not as good as writing once.

Harmonious Qi,

Master Zhongxian Wu and Dr. Karin Taylor Wu
Year of the Yin Water Snake, Middle Summer
Phoenix Nest, Stockholm's archipelago, Sweden

瑞　癸　吳　吳
典　巳　簫　忠
鳳　仲　玲　賢
棲　夏
巢

癸巳仲夏吉日
乾元手 於瑞典

1

TongTianShenShu 通天神樹

Mystical Tree of Heaven

In this chapter, we will introduce some background information and stress the basic principles that will bring context to *XiangShu* 象數, the symbolism and numerology of each Heavenly Stem and Earthly Branch. Please take your time to review this section before moving on to the rest of the book.

Figure 1: Paper rubbing of the Magic Tree from a Han Dynasty era stone carving

1.1 The Way of Heaven and Earth

TianGan 天干 (Heavenly Stems) and *DiZhi* 地支 (Earthly Branches) are commonly abbreviated GanZhi 干支. The GanZhi originated in the ancient Chinese cosmological sciences and a complex calendrical system created to codify the patterns of the universe. For thousands of years, small groups of Chinese shaman-kings, sages, scholars, doctors, astronomers, cosmologists, and politicians have used the GanZhi symbols as sacred tools that unlock the fundamental nature of reality. During the Shang Dynasty (1700–1027 BCE—one of the longest running dynasties in China's history), which marked great advancements in agriculture, astronomy, bronze casting, music, sculpture, and written communication, the Emperors regarded themselves as the sons of

Heaven and took the GanZhi symbols as their own names. For thousands of years, it has been held that those who master the knowledge of the GanZhi system hold the keys to the sublime.

Figure 2: The round and square shaped ruins of NiuHeLiang 牛河梁, *a Neolithic archaeological site from about 5000 years ago, were discovered in LiaoNing* 遼寧 *province in 1983 and suggest early Chinese cosmographies of the Heavenly Way and Earthly Way.*

1.1.1 TianGan 天干 Heavenly Stems

In Chinese, *Tian* 天 means day, sky, heaven, and universe; *Gan* 干 means the trunk or stem of a plant, dry, deed, do, work, hold, or take action. In classical Chinese, *Gan* 干 is also depicted as the following symbols: 幹 (meaning the stem of a plant); 簳 (an object displayed on a stick so that it may be seen clearly); or 乾 (dry, or the name of the trigram and hexagram "Heaven" in Yijing/I Ching—*Book of Change*). *TianGan* means "Heavenly Stem" and invokes the image of a giant tree trunk connecting heaven and earth.

TianGan is a traditional Chinese term that represents a specific group of ten Chinese characters: Jia甲, Yi 乙, Bing 丙, Ding 丁, Wu 戊, Ji 己, Geng 庚, Xin 辛, Ren 壬, and Gui 癸. These ten symbols embody *TianDao* 天道— the Way of Heaven. *TianDao* means circular, circle, round, spin, spiral, and continuous movement.

Figure 3: The Heavenly Way of TianGan

1.1.2 DiZhi 地支 Earthly Branches

Di 地 means earth, ground, terrain, and place; *Zhi* 支 means the branch or twig of a tree or a plant, support, supply, assist, treat with, defend, or forked area. *Zhi* 支 can be written as the character 枝, which also means the branch of a plant. *DiZhi* means "Earthly Branch" and draws to mind the intricate system of branches connected to the giant trunk of *TianGan*.

Similar to *TianGan*, *DiZhi* is a Chinese term that contains a collection of twelve specific Chinese characters: Zi 子, Chou 丑, Yin 寅, Mao 卯, Chen 辰, Si 巳, Wu 午, Wei 未, Shen 申, You 酉, Xü 戌, and Hai 亥. *DiZhi* represents *DiDao* 地道, the Way of Earth. *DiDao* means square, corner, stable, solid, keeping still, and without movement.

Figure 4: The Earthly Way of DiZhi

1.2 The Origin of GanZhi

As mentioned in my book, *The Vital Breath of the Dao*,[1] archaeological evidence indicates that possible precursors to Chinese characters appeared 8000 years ago. Unearthed inscriptions found on scapulae and tortoise shells verify that a complete system of Chinese written language was in use during the Shang Dynasty (1700–1027 BCE). The inscriptions were related to the divination practices of the Shang emperors and the distinctive style of Chinese character used in them is called *JiaGuWen* 甲骨文—Oracle Script.

The earliest known written record of the Stems and Branches exists in these ancient "oracle bones." For centuries (or more), traditional Chinese medicine doctors used the oracle bones as *LongGu* 龍骨 or dragon bones—a common ingredient in Chinese herbal medicine formulas— yet it wasn't until the early 20th century that their historical significance became clear. This exciting discovery confirmed the historical truth of the Shang Dynasty, which had previously been questioned among various scholars. Through archaeological evidence, we can confirm that the Stems and Branches have been in use in Chinese imperial calendrical and divination systems at least since the reign of the Shang Dynasty emperors.

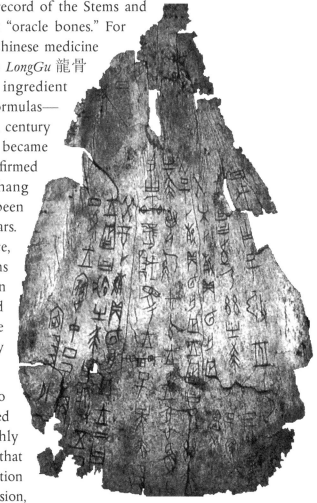

As yet, no one has been able to definitively ascertain who invented the Heavenly Stems and Earthly Branches. It is commonly held that they existed long before the invention of the Chinese characters. One version, prevalent within the field of traditional Chinese Yijing prediction, relates that

Figure 5: GanZhi in oracle bone script (Shang Dynasty)

1 Wu, Master Zhongxian (2008) *Vital Breath of the Dao: Chinese Shamanic Tiger Qigong—Laohu Gong.* London: Singing Dragon.

Heaven released the ten Stems on *YuanQiu* 圓丘 (Rotund Hill) during the time of *HuangDi* 黃帝, the Yellow Emperor, who is traditionally believed to have lived in 2700–2600 BCE. In order to understand the Way of Heaven and follow the rhythm of nature, the Yellow Emperor instructed his minister, DaRao 大橈 to create twelve complimentary Branches to complete the JiaZi 甲子. The JiaZi is the Chinese calendar, named after Jia 甲, the first Stem and Zi 子, the first Branch, and it is made up solely of these Stems and Branches. The Han Dynasty author, SiMa Qian 司馬遷 (140 BCE–220 CE), who wrote *ShiJi* 史記 (The Book of History), maintains that it was indeed the Yellow Emperor who invented the Stem and Branch system for the purpose of creating the Chinese calendar. Other books, such as *WuXing DaYi* 五行大義 (The Great Meaning of Five Elements) and *YueLing ZhangJu* 月令章句 (Interpretation on Monthly Commander), credit DaRao for creating the Stem and Branch system and Chinese calendar.

1.3 The Magic Tree

We can also look to mythology to find possible origins of the GanZhi. The ancient Chinese book of mythology, *ShanHaiJing* 山海經 (*The Canon of Mountains and Seas*, which has existed since the 4th century BCE), contains the following mythological roots of the GanZhi:

生 帝 生 帝 義
月 俊 十 俊 和
十 妻 日 之 者
有 常 … 妻
二 義

XiHeZhe DiJunZhiQi ShengShiRi…
DiJunQiChangXi ShengYueShiYouEr

The ten Heavenly Stems are related with the ten Suns story:
There is *XiHe* 義和, the wife of Emperor Jun 俊,
who gave birth to ten Suns…

And the twelve Earthly Branches are related to the twelve Moons story:
The Emperor Jun 俊 married ChangXi 常義,
who gave birth to twelve Moons.

Figure 6: ChangXi 常義 bathing the twelve moons may symbolize her creation of the systematized method of tracking the timing of the twelve lunar month cycles. China has a long history of using water to count time.

According to Chinese mythology, Emperor Jun was a supreme deity who ruled over the ten Suns and twelve Moons. Ancient Chinese regarded his two wives, XiHe and ChangXi, as the Goddess of Sun and the Goddess of Moon. The story of XiHe giving birth to the ten Suns could be interpreted as XiHe creating the Chinese solar calendar, which is based on ten-day cycles and the ten Heavenly Stems. In Chinese, the written character *Ri* 日 can be used to mean both sun and day, and the ten-day-cycle is called *Xun* 旬. Although the concept is not popular today in modern cities, in the countryside, Chinese people living close to the land and rhythms of nature still use *Xun* in daily life.

Similarly, the Chinese character *Yue* 月 is used to mean both moon and month. ChangXi gave birth to the twelve Moons (twelve Earthly Branches) of the lunar calendar.

Another significant connection between the GanZhi and Chinese mythology is the tree. In China, there are two legendary magic trees, *JianMu* 建木 and *FuSang* 扶桑. According to the *ShanHaiJing*, the Yellow Emperor himself planted *JianMu,* whereas *FuSang* grows in *TangGu* 湯谷, the place where the ten Suns bathe. Chinese know each of these trees as *TongTianShu* 通天樹, which means "the tree providing the way to heaven." According to tradition, remarkable human beings are able to climb these trees to communicate with the heavenly realm.

The primary symbolic image of GanZhi is that of a tree—the tree of life. In Chinese tradition, a tree connects heaven and earth (as does humanity) and represents strong life energy. Over many years, we have used our knowledge of the GanZhi to guide our spiritual cultivation and clinical practice. We have come to realize that *Gan* and *Zhi*, the Heavenly Stems and Earthly Branches, are in fact *TongTianShu*—the magic trees, *JianMu* and *FuSang*.

In 1986, a representation of *FuSang* in the form of a Bronze Tree of Heaven (also known as the Bronze Magic Tree) was unearthed from *SanXingDui* 三星堆 (Three Stars' Mound) in *SiChuan* 四川 province, China. This amazing archaeological discovery sparked news around the world and established the existence of large-scale sculptures from the middle of the Shang Dynasty (radiocarbon dating places the origin of the tree in the 12th–11th centuries BCE). In what is believed to have been two large sacrificial pits of the ancient *Shu* 屬 people (*Shu* is the original name of *SiChuan*), large amounts of bronze wares, gold wares, jade wares, ivories, shells, and earthenware were uncovered. Among the most impressive were large bronze human figures with exaggerated features, wearing gold masks (one of which is the world's largest and best preserved upright bronze human figure), as well as bronze animal-faced sculptures, bells, axes, and decorative animals like dragons, snakes, chicks, and birds, as well as tables, masks and belts of gold, and jade axes, tablets, rings, knives and tubes. From the viewpoint of one of my masters, Professor Wang JiaYou 王家祐 (an archaeologist and Daoist scholar), the artifacts were sacrifices from the ancient King of *Shu* to the Queen Mother of the West, the ancestral master of Daoism, who resided in the legendary *KunLun* 崑崙 Mountains.

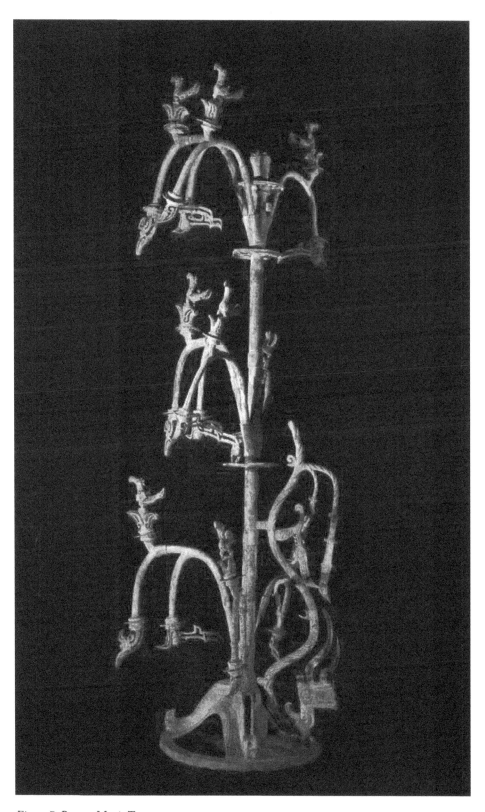

Figure 7: Bronze Magic Tree

The trunk of the Bronze Tree of Heaven is 3.84m (12.6ft) in height and sits on a three-mountain-peak shaped base. With the top missing, the whole sculpture now stands at 3.96m (13ft) and archaeologists believe that it would have stood at 5m (16.4ft) with the top intact. The tree is composed of three sections. Each layer has three arched branches with a bird perched on the top of each bend.

Though there are a total of nine birds on the tree, it is commonly held that the tenth bird is either on the missing top or off flying in the sky performing its duty. The ten birds represent the ten Suns. In Chinese mythology, there were ten suns in the sky and each had a black bird living inside of it. The *FuSang* tree was their home. Each day, one sun would fly into the sky shedding light on the earth and its inhabitants while the others would rest in the tree, until the day HouYi 後羿 the archer shot nine of them down.

In each section of the tree, one branch is forked at the bend (making a total of four arched branches in each section) and at the end of each arched branch there is a round-shaped fruit. There are a total of twelve fruits on the tree, which represent the twelve Moons. A dragon spirals down the trunk of the tree. The dragon symbolizes great transformation, the way to connect heaven and earth, and

Figure 8: Bronze tree, bird detail

Figure 9: Bronze tree, dragon detail

the Eastern Green Dragon, which in ancient times was also used as a reference to mark the passage of time.

It is our interpretation that the ten birds of this tree represent the ten-day cycles of the sun and the ten Heavenly Stems, and the twelve fruits depict the twelve lunar cycles of the year and the twelve Earthly Branches. Therefore, we regard this Bronze Tree of Heaven artifact as an ancient symbol of GanZhi—the tree of Stems and Branches.

We invite you to "climb to Heaven" with us, discover the Dao, and walk the path of awareness and self-healing so that we may benefit others. We hope this book will help you use the GanZhi, the keys to the sublime, to master ancient Chinese wisdom traditions.

1.4 Celestial Connection of GanZhi

In the old tradition, knowledge of the GanZhi is believed to have come directly from the heavens—GanZhi are intrinsically entwined with the stars that speckle the night sky. Please allow us to briefly introduce the way ancient Chinese studied the sky before we move forward and discuss the celestial connection to GanZhi.

Figure 10: A color painting of the sky, containing the 28 lunar mansions and the Babylonian zodiac, on the ceiling of a Liao Dynasty tomb in XuanHua 宣化, HeBei 河北 province

Ancient Chinese astronomers divided the entire sky into 31 regions, three of which were regarded as the center of the sky, radiating around the Polar Star. The remaining 28 regions are distributed along *HuangDao* 黄道 (Yellow Belt)—the ecliptic. The ecliptic is the path of the Sun on the celestial sphere as discernable from the Earth's center. Each of these regions is dominated by one *Xiu* 宿 along the ecliptic. Conceptually, *Xiu* is similar to what we call constellation in the Western world. The smallest *Xiu* is made up of two stars while the largest one contains 22 stars. In English, these 28 *Xiu* are commonly known as the 28 Lunar Mansions.

Figure 11: Lunar Mansions and Twelve Animals painting by Xiao YunCong 蕭雲従
(1596–1673 CE)

Given that the *Xiu* mark the daily position of the Moon during its monthly orbit around Earth, we find that the Moon resides in a different Lunar Mansion each night. Chinese astronomers observed each quadrant of the sky (found in the four cardinal directions) and found that every seven Mansions form a clear pattern—that of a spiritual animal.

Figure 12: Tang Dynasty bronze mirror with four spiritual animals

The four spiritual animals are *QingLong* 青龍, the Green Dragon on the eastern sky, *XuanWu* 玄武, the Mystical Warrior (turtle and snake) in the north, *BaiHu* 白虎, the White Tiger to the west, and *ZhuQue* 朱雀, the southern Red Bird. Table 1 lists the four spiritual animals with their associated Lunar Mansions.

Table 1: Four spiritual animals and 28 Lunar Mansions

Direction	East	North	West	South
Spiritual Animal	*QingLong* 青龍 Green Dragon	*XuanWu* 玄武 Mystical Warrior	*BaiHu* 白虎 White Tiger	*ZhuQue* 朱雀 Red Bird
Xiu 宿 **Lunar Mansions**	*Jiao* 角 Horn	*Dou* 斗 Little Dipper	*Kui* 奎 Thigh	*Jing* 井 Well
	Kang 亢 Neck	*Niu* 牛 Ox	*Lou* 婁 Basket	*Gui* 鬼 Ghost
	Di 氐 Root	*Nü* 女 Weaving Girl	*Wei* 胃 Stomach	*Liu* 柳 Willow
	Fang 房 Chamber	*Xü* 虛 Void	*Mao* 昴 Prosper	*Xing* 星 Star
	Xin 心 Heart	*Wei* 危 Cliff	*Bi* 畢 Accomplishment	*Zhang* 張 Spread
	Wei 尾 Tail	*Shi* 室 Room	*Zi* 觜 Beak	*Yi* 翼 Wing
	Ji 箕 Winnowing Basket	*Bi* 壁 Wall	*Shen* 參 March	*Zhen* 軫 Chariot

The 28 Lunar Mansions have the following associations with the Heavenly Stems: Jia 甲 and Yi 乙 with the eastern Green Dragon; Bing 丙 and Ding 丁 with the southern Red Bird; Geng 庚 and Xin 辛 with western White Tiger; and Ren 壬 and Gui 癸 with northern Mystical Warrior. The other two Heavenly Stems, Wu 戊 and Ji 己, are associated with the central celestial region. We will provide more information about each Heavenly Stem and its related Lunar Mansion in Chapter 2.

With respect to the Earthly Branches, Yin 寅, Mao 卯, and Chen 辰 are connected to the eastern Green Dragon; Si 巳, Wu 午, and Wei 未 are related to southern Red Bird; Shen 申, You 酉, and Xü 戌 are associated with the western White Tiger; and Hai 亥, Zi 子, and Chou 丑 are linked with the northern Mystical Warrior.

Table 2: Four spiritual animals, Heavenly Stems and Earthly Branches

Direction	East	North	West	South
Spiritual Animal	*QingLong* 青龍 Green Dragon	*XuanWu* 玄武 Mystical Warrior	*BaiHu* 白虎 White Tiger	*ZhuQue* 朱雀 Red Bird
Heavenly Stems	Jia 甲 Yi 乙	Ren 壬 Gui 癸	Geng 庚 Xin 辛	Bing 丙 Ding 丁
Earthly Branches	Yin 寅 Mao 卯 Chen 辰	Si 巳 Wu 午 Wei 未	Shen 申 You 酉 Xü 戌	Hai 亥 Zi 子 Chou 丑

Originally, the function of the Chinese ideogram was not reserved for communication between human beings. The saying *WenYiZaiDao* 文以載道—the pattern carries the Dao—reveals the purpose of the Chinese characters as vehicles for connecting with nature and channeling universal wisdom. Studying Chinese graphemes, particularly Oracle Script, the oldest known Chinese written pattern, can provide us with insight into the wisdom of the ancient Chinese sages. Thus, with the *Gan* (ten Heavenly Stems) and *Zhi* (twelve Earthly Branches) we gain greater understanding of the connection between GanZhi and Chinese star constellations if we carefully study the ancient written character of each Heavenly Stem and Earthly Branch. We will do this together in Chapters 2 and 3 of this book.

Figure 13: Harmonizing the four spiritual animals from the Daoist internal alchemy book XingMingGuiZhi 性命圭旨

1.5 GanZhi YinYang 陰陽

YinYang is the most basic and central philosophical and practical concept in all Chinese wisdom traditions. Chapter 5 of *HuangDiNeiJing* (the primary classical text of Chinese medicine) gives us insight into YinYang:

神 生 變 萬 天
明 殺 化 物 地 陰
之 之 之 之 之 陽
府 本 父 綱 道 者
也 始 母 紀 也

YinYangZhe
TianDiZhiDaoYe
WanWuZhiGangJi
BianHuZhiFuMu
ShengSha ZhiBenShi
ShenMingZhiFuYe

YinYang
which is the Way of Heaven and Earth
is the law and the principle of Ten-Thousand-
Things [everything in existence]
is the parent of changing and transformation
is the initiation and termination of birth and death
and is the home of Spiritual Brightness [high consciousness or wisdom].

The qualities of Yin are feminine, shady, stillness, conservation, inward, descending, withdrawn, hidden, unknown, condensed, nourishing, and more. The qualities of Yang include masculine, brightness, movement, consuming, outward, ascending, forward, exposing, clarity, expending, and wasted. Table 3 gives some examples to help you get a conceptual feeling for Yin and Yang.

Table 3: Yin and Yang generalizations

Yin	Yang
Earth	Heaven
Zhi	Gan
Night	Day
Not clear	Clear
Woman	Man
Black	White
Cold	Hot
Front of your body	Back of your body
Lower body	Upper body

Now that you have a feeling for Yin and Yang, please remember that YinYang are actually an inseparable pair. In the beginning, to distill the essence of Yin and Yang, we identify predominantly Yin or Yang qualities of an object, as listed in Table 3. However, there will always be an element of the YinYang pair within any object, any energy, any time period, and any spatial relationship. For a simple example of this, we can look to our own bodies. Table 3 shows that the front side of your body is Yin in relation to the back side of your body and that the lower half of your body is Yin compared with the upper half of your body. Of course the back side of your body (Yang) has both an upper (Yang) and lower (Yin) half. The back side of your upper body is Yang within Yang and the back side of your lower body is Yin within Yang. Similarly, the front side (Yin) of your body has an upper (Yang) and lower (Yin) half, so the front side of your upper body is Yang within Yin and the front side of your lower body is Yin within Yin. Yin energy necessarily contains Yang within, just as Yang energy necessarily contains Yin energy within. As Confucius states in *XiCi* 繫詞, one of his commentaries on the Yijing: *YiYinYiYangZhiWeiDao* 一陰一陽之謂道—The interaction between Yin and Yang is called the Dao.

Equality in the exchange of forces between Yin and Yang generates an alternating, balanced state of an object, an event, in timing or in space. An excess of either Yin or Yang will disrupt this balance. When the energy becomes maximally imbalanced towards Yin and Yin reaches its most extreme point, Yin will give birth to Yang. Equally, when Yang reaches its zenith, it will generate Yin. To help make this concept clear, we can look at what happens in nature. In Chinese, the spring and autumn equinoxes are known as the YinYang balance points of the yearly cycle. The hours of daylight in a 24-hour period are moderate. On the other hand, the winter and summer solstice mark the climax of Yin and Yang energy. On these days, we experience the fewest (or greatest) number of hours of sunlight. The solstices also represent the turning point in the cycle, where extreme Yin becomes Yang (the light starts to return) and Yang becomes Yin (the light begins to recede). Like the patterns of energy that we observe in the cycles of nature, the relationship between Yin and Yang are constantly in flux. The dynamic change between Yin and Yang is the inner driving force of life and it is the momentum of the Dao.

Traditionally, GanZhi are used to illustrate the Five Elements' Yin and Yang nature. Of the pair, *Gan* is Yang and *Zhi* is Yin. As Yang is clear and straightforward, delineating Yin and Yang Heavenly Stems is also straightforward. First, we must learn the correct order of Gan, the ten Heavenly Stems: Jia 甲, Yi 乙, Bing 丙, Ding 丁, Wu 戊, Ji 己, Geng 庚, Xin 辛, Ren 壬, and Gui 癸. Using this order, the YinYang pattern is clear: Jia 甲 represents Yang energy, the next stem, Yi 乙, represents Yin energy. This alternating pattern continues in the same predictable way through the entire set of ten. Table 4 shows the Yin and Yang Heavenly Stems.

Table 4: Yin and Yang Heavenly Stems

Yin	Yang
Yi 乙	Jia 甲
Ding 丁	Bing 丙
Ji 己	Wu 戊
Xin 辛	Geng 庚
Gui 癸	Ren 壬

Yin, on the other hand, is dark and rather mysterious. It follows that determining the YinYang characteristics of each Earthly Branch is more complex—there are three classification systems to keep in mind and when classifying the Earthly Branches it is important to remain clear about your purpose. You will notice that each Branch may be classified as both Yin and Yang, depending on the context.

You will remember from our previous discussion that Yin and Yang are never truly separated. In Chapter 42 of the *DaoDeJing*, LaoZi says: *WangWuFuYinErBaoYang* 萬物負陰而抱陽—everything that exists holds both the Yin and Yang.

As with the Heavenly Stems, the first step is to learn the correct order of the Earthly Branches: Zi 子, Chou 丑, Yin 寅, Mao 卯, Chen 辰, Si 巳, Wu 午, Wei 未, Shen 申, You 酉, Xü 戌, and Hai 亥. Next, apply the following systematization:

1. **According to the natural daily and monthly cycles:** Yang Qi, or Yang energy, gains strength for 12 hours in each daily rhythm, mounting in strength from 23:00 to 11:00. Yin Qi, or Yin energy, also escalates for 12 hours of each 24-hour period, from 11:00 to 23:00. The first six Branches (Zi 子, Chou 丑, Yin 寅, Mao 卯, Chen 辰, and Si 巳) correlate with the rising tide of Yang Qi. The last six Branches (Wu 午, Wei 未, Shen 申, You 酉, Xü 戌, and Hai 亥) are Yin and are expressions of swelling Yin Qi. We also use the natural monthly cycles (starting with Zi 子, the month of the winter solstice) to determine YinYang qualities of the Branches. You can see the waxing and waning of the YinYang energy in Figure 14—the hours of the Chinese clock and the solstices have been included for added context.

Figure 14: DiZhi waxing and waning pattern of YinYang

2. **According to numeric order:** In traditional Chinese philosophy, odd numbers are considered to have Yang qualities and even numbers are regarded as Yin. Consequently, Zi 子, Yin 寅, Chen 辰, Wu 午,

Shen 申, and Xü 戌 are each Yang because they are the odd numbered Earthly Branches: 1, 3, 5, 7, 9, and 11. Chou 丑, Mao 卯, Si 巳, We 未, You 酉, and Hai 亥 are Yin because they correlate with the even number Earthly Branches: 2, 4, 6, 8, 10, and 12. Please note that when we are working specifically with the Chinese calendar, we apply *only* this numerological YinYang classification to the Earthly Branches.

3. **According to the individual energetic quality of each Branch, as related to the annual cycles of nature**: Yin 寅, Shen 申, Si 巳, and Hai 亥 are Yang and are the initial energy of the four seasons and four directions. Zi 子, Wu 午, Mao 卯, and You 酉 are Yin and are the dominant central energy of four seasons and four directions. Chen 辰 and Xü 戌 are Yang, whereas Chou 丑 and Wei 未 are Yin. These four mark the transitioning or ending energy of four seasons and four directions. This is the method we use to identify YinYang energies of each Earthly Branch when we analyze Chinese astrology, make cosmological forecasts, and use Yijing prediction systems.

Table 5: Method 3—Determining Earthly Branch YinYang energies

Season and Direction Stage	Spring/ East	Summer/ South	Autumn/ West	Winter/ North
Beginning (Yang)	Yin 寅	Si 巳	Shen 申	Hai 亥
Middle (Yin)	Mao 卯	Wu 午	You 酉	Zi 子
Transition/End	Chen 辰	Wei 未	Xü 戌	Chou 丑

1.6 GanZhi *WuXing* 五行

WuXing 五行, the fundamental Daoist philosophy of Five Elements, plays a role in traditional Chinese culture that is as vital as the YinYang principle. All things and phenomena in the universe are composed of the Five Elements: Water 水, Wood 木, Fire 火, Earth 土, and Metal 金. In turn, each Element has both Yin and Yang aspects, and throughout history the Heavenly Stems and Earthly Branches have been used to exemplify the Yin and Yang qualities of the Elements.

WuXing is commonly translated as Five Elements, although Five Phases may be more accurate. However, in this case we will adhere to convention and use the familiar translation. Grasping the intricacies of *WuXing* and its principles, even for most native Chinese, can be taxing. As Confucius justly said (again, from the *XiCi* 繫詞): *BaiXingRiYongErBuZhi, GuJunZiZhiDaoXieYi* 百姓日用而不知 故君子之道鮮矣—common people use it every day yet do not understand the reasoning. The knowledge of the Dao is rarely understood, save for small groups of enlightened beings.

Let us spend a little time studying some information about *Wu* 五 and *Xing* 行, in an effort to better assimilate the basic Five Elements principles we will explore later.

Wu 五, the modern Chinese character for the number five, is derived from an oracle bone ideogram that shows two horizontal lines, representing heaven above and earth below, connected by two intersecting diagonal lines—Yin and Yang energies dancing together, intertwined between heaven and earth. According to the 2nd century Chinese dictionary, *ShuoWenJieZhi* 說文解字, *Wu* 五 means Ten-Thousand-Things dancing together.

Figure 15: Early Oracle Script for Wu 五—Five

Xing 行 means walk, move, act, cross, job, or phase. Its progenitor Oracle Script character is an image of an intersection. In ancient time, intersections served as the main market place—the original "World Trade Centers." People from the four directions (in classical Chinese, "four directions" means everywhere) would gather in the center (the intersection) to buy, sell, and trade all manner of goods. The true meaning of *Xing* is the interaction between and among the different Elements.

From Master Wu:

I grew up in a remote area of southern China, long before modernization (meaning electricity, piped water, bicycles, automobiles, and paved roads) finally reached our traditional fishing village. Until the 1980s, our daily lifestyle had remained unchanged for centuries, perhaps for even thousands of years. I have fond memories of the happenings in our main village intersection.

Every day, especially during the morning hours, street venders from local and surrounding villages would gather goods and hawk their wares. Fresh vegetables, fish, meat, and other sundries lined the edges of our small flagstone intersection, leaving a small narrow walking path down the middle. The constant motion of shoppers (predominantly women) and young children flooded the narrow lane. Stray dogs lurked, seizing upon the opportunities presented by a momentarily turned head or distracted young one to grab a bite for themselves. As the day progressed, activity would lull and by dinnertime, the intersection would become fairly quiet for a spell. Gradually, after the evening meal, men would gather in the intersection for having a chat, trading vital information about current fishing conditions, or working out the newest location of nightfall's "secret casino." At that time, gambling remained an important social event despite having been deemed illegal after Chairman Mao's new government was established in 1949.

Figure 16: Oracle Script for Xing 行—*Element*

By definition, *Xing* has action or movement implied and, as such, each Element is never considered a fixed thing or object. We haven chosen to capitalize Water, Wood, Fire, Earth, and Metal when referring to *WuXing* to distinguish them from ordinary elements. Each Element is a conglomerate of symbols representing the universal way, including time, space, color, flavor, odor, organ, anatomy, musical tone, and emotion.

Among the ten Heavenly Stems, Jia and Yi are classified as belonging to the Wood Element; Bing and Ding to Fire; Wu 戊 and Ji to Earth; Geng and Xin to Metal; and Ren and Gui to Water.

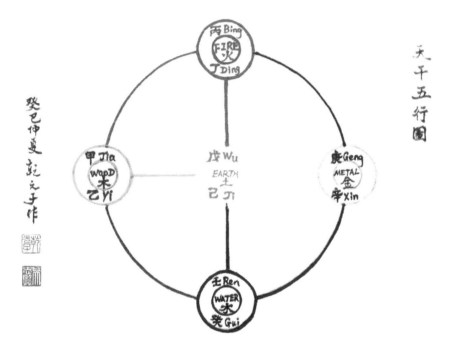

Figure 17: Heavenly Stems Five Elements Diagram

The twelve Earthly Branches are grouped into YinYang pairs of Elements— Yin 寅 and Mao are Wood; Si and Wu 午 are Fire; Chen, Xü, Chou, and Wei are Earth; Shen and You are Metal; and Hai and Zi are Water.

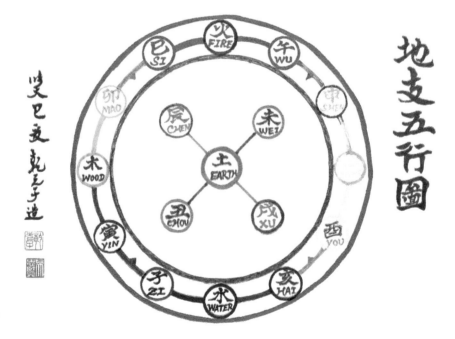

Figure 18: Earthly Branches Five Elements Diagram

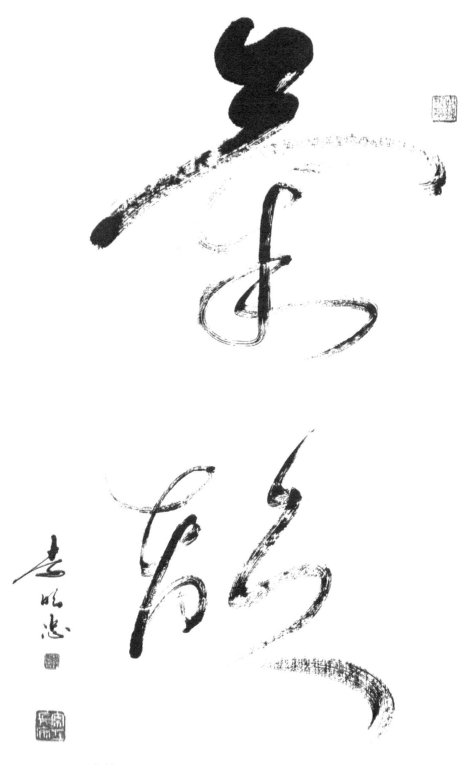

Figure 19: QiYun 氣韵 *(Rhythm of Qi) calligraphy by Master Li MingZhong, renowned Qin musician and classical Chinese music scholar*

1.7 *QiYun* 氣韻 The Rhythm of Qi

In classical Chinese philosophy and Daoist tradition, we have used the musical scale to describe and measure different qualities of Qi within nature and our bodies for thousands of years. The ancient sages and enlightened beings understood the fluctuation

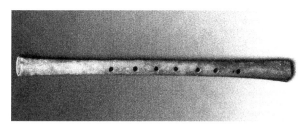

Figure 20: Musical scale bone pipe/flute with seven holes that is over 7000 years old, excavated from the ancient ruin JiaHu 賈湖 *in HeNan* 河南 *province*

of the patterns of nature's *QiYun* 氣韻—rhythm of Qi—as peaceful songs. The peaceful song, or harmonious sound, was a way to represent the human being living in harmony with nature, and served as a seasonal guide to this pursuit. This ultimate goal has been named *TianRenHeYi* 天人合一 (the union between human being and nature) since at least the Warring States period, circa 475–221 BCE.

The Heavenly Stems and Earthly Branches are the "musical notes" that are used to perform the song of nature. The Ten Stems are associated with *WuYin* 五音, the Chinese pentatonic scale (with five notes per octave), which is the fundamental scale of classical Chinese musical compositions. The five *WuYin* are *Gong* 宮, *Shang* 商, *Jue* 角, *Zhi* 徵, and *Yü* 羽. *Gong* 宮 represents the Earth Element and also corresponds to the first musical note, C or Do, of the widely known heptatonic scale (the musical scale with seven pitches per octave—C, D, E, F, G, A, and B). *Shang* 商 designates the Metal Element and is the same musical note as the second tone of the heptatonic scale, D or Re; *Jue* 角 stands for the Wood Element (E or Mi); *Zhi* 徵, the Fire Element (G or So); and *Yü* 羽 (the Water Element) is A or La.

Gong is in charge of the Stems Jia and Ji; *Shang* is in charge of Yi and Geng; *Jue* is in charge of Ding and Ren; *Zhi* is in charge of Wu 戊 and Gui; and *Yü* is in charge of Bing and Xin.

Figure 21: WuYin and Stems Diagram

In Chinese cosmology, we use the Stems to decode their related musical scale so that we may accurately forecast the weather patterns and their effects on the body. Please read Section 4.6 *WuYun* 五運 Five Cosmological Energies for more details.

The twelve Earthly Branches are associated with *LüLü* 律呂, a standardized twelve-pitch scale. Unique to ancient Chinese music, this chromatic scale is a series of fundamental notes from which scales themselves were constructed. This Chinese scale uses the same intervals as the Pythagorean scale, which is also based on 2:3 ratios.

It has been said that in the Yellow Emperor's time, the famous Chinese musician LingLun 伶倫 discovered *LüLü*. LingLun made twelve different sized pipes according to 2:3 ratios, filled them with reed ash and buried one side underground at the foot of *KunLun* 崑崙 Mountain. Every month, the earthly Qi would blow ash from one of the pipes and would make a special musical sound. LingLun recorded the sounds and gave them different names: *HuangZhong* 黃鐘, *DaLü* 大呂, *TaiCu* 太簇, *JiaZhong* 夾鐘, *GuXian* 姑洗, *ZhongLü* 仲呂, *RuiBin* 蕤賓, *LinZhong* 林鐘, *YiZe* 夷則, *NanLü* 南呂, *WuYi* 無射, and *YingZhong* 應鐘—these are the twelve notes of the *LüLü*.

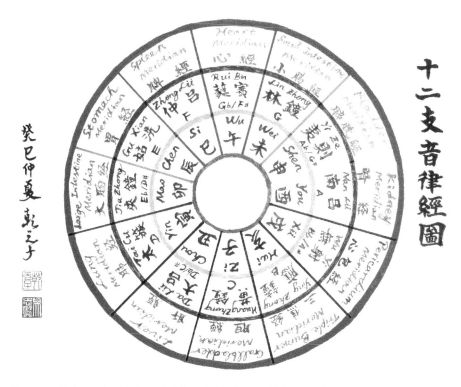

Figure 22: LüLü—Earthly Branch, Musical Rhythm, and Meridian Diagram

Each note of the *LüLü* describes the quality of Qi and energetic frequency of the twelve months of the annual cycle. *LüLü* is also used to illustrate the daily rhythm of the twelve bi-hours of the Chinese clock. Within the human body, these same twelve *LüLü* Qi exist as the twelve main acupuncture meridians. The relationships between each Earthly Branch, its *LüLü* and associated meridian are depicted in Figure 22. There is more information about each *LüLü* in its corresponding Branch section in Chapter 3, *DiZhi XiangShu* 地支象數 Earthly Branch Symbolism.

In JiaZi, the Sexagenary Cycle of GanZhi, each combination of Stem and Branch has its own Five Element musical rhythm, or *NaYinWuXing* 納音五行 (see section 4.13 *LiuShiHuaJia* 六十花甲 Sixty Stem Branch Combinations), which are commonly used to measure the yearly energetic pattern of nature. In *DaSanYuan* 大三元 (Great Three Sources) style FengShui, we use the Sexagenary Cycle as the basic unit to characterize the different quality of Qi of the natural or living environment, which can be calculated over very long periods of time, from thousands of years ago to thousands of years to come.

The natural rhythm of Qi is like a peaceful song and the musical system of Stems and Branches is a traditional way to measure and evaluate the energetic patterns of nature and of your body.

天干象数

癸巳仲夏吉日
乾之手於瑞典

2

TianGan XiangShu 天干象數

Heavenly Stems Symbolism

In this chapter, we will focus on *XiangShu* 象數, the symbolism and numerology of the ten Heavenly Stems. *XiangShu* contains the vital essence of the Daoist Yijing (I Ching) system. This information is ubiquitous throughout traditional Chinese arts, and is used as medicine in its own right, as guiding principles of medical practice, to strengthen the body's innate ability to restore health, to support others on their healing journey, to deepen our inner cultivation, and to create harmonious FengShui 風水 (the art of understanding cosmological and geological influences on our vitality and prosperity).

Modern people have difficulties comprehending ancient languages and concepts. This is especially true of the meanings of *XiangShu* as they are far outside the realm of logical thinking and the daily lives of most people. Therefore, we will provide our commentary throughout the rest of the book to explain the hidden meanings within the Stems and Branches. The Five Element qualities of the Heavenly Stems are the most challenging aspect of *XiangShu*. If you find yourself struggling to understand the Five Element and Stem correlations, please take time to study the fundamental Five Elements principles laid out for you in Chapter 4.

2.1 Jia 甲

Jia 甲 means shell, armor, helmet, fingernail, toenail, claw, and scale. It is the first Heavenly Stem and represents the number one, the top, and the best.

The Oracle Script for Jia resembles a cross, and we believe that this ancient character was created in the image of the first eastern Lunar Mansion *Jiao* 角 and another asterism, *PingDao* 平道 (Peace Path). *Jiao* means horn, corner, and antler. *Jiao*, as the first of the 28 Lunar Mansions and the starting point of Chinese celestial orbits, is also called *TianJue* 天闕 or Heavenly Gateway. *Jiao* contains two stars which straddle the ecliptic, the apparent pathway of the sun as seen from the Earth's center. Along the central line of these two stars there are another two stars known as *PingDao* 平道. *PingDao* runs parallel with the ecliptic. When we intersect imaginary lines drawn between the two stars of *Jiao* and *PingDao*, we can see the cross pattern of the Oracle Script for Jia.

Figure 23: Star pattern—the source of the 甲 *character*

Element: YangMu 陽木 Yang Wood

Yang Wood has straight and direct qualities and represents the power of life.

Spiritual Animal: *QingLong* 青龍 Green Dragon

Spiritual animals are important totems in many Chinese traditions. The spiritual animals of Heavenly Stems are the same as those of the four directions and central spirit.

Green is the color of eastern Qi (vital energy) and the Dragon is a symbol for ascension, new life energy, and great transformation. The Green Dragon is represented in the seven eastern Lunar Mansions. It is also the totem of the ancient tribes of eastern China. In Daoist inner cultivation practices, the Dragon represents rising energy and free flowing Qi.

五九 芦山王晖石棺青龙图

Figure 24: Paper rubbing of the Green Dragon from a Han Dynasty era stone carving

Season: *MengChun* 孟春 Early Spring

Jia Wood also correlates with early spring Yang Qi and with the return of new life energy in nature. Jia's early spring energy also refers to the early springtime (most of February and early March) in the annual cycle, the hours of the early morning, as well as any time when strong life energy appears in a life cycle, as in early childhood.

Direction: *Dong* 東 East

Similar to the season, the direction of a Stem does not have a singular fixed meaning. Jia originates in the eastern Qi and symbolizes the spiritual direction of east. This spiritual eastern direction may mean the actual directions of east or northeast, and can also be the left side your body or your home.

Trigram: ☳ *Zhen* 震 Thunder

The trigram *Zhen* is made with one Yang line on the bottom and two Yin lines on top. It portrays Yang Qi, or new life energy rising, shaking off the Yin Qi or old energy. Among others, *Zhen* also has the symbolic meanings of thunder, older son, shake, foot, and dragon. For more detailed information about the symbolic meaning of each of the trigrams, please read Chapter 4 "*Xiang* 象: Symbolism" in *Seeking the Spirit of The Book of Change.*[1]

Body: Gallbladder, head, scapula, thyroid, nervous system, ankle, fingernails, toenails

Jia can represent any of the body parts listed above. Understanding this kind information helps shape our Chinese astrology chart analysis, Yijing diagnosis, and skills as a medical practitioner. We have added the commentary in this section of each stem to help prepare the advanced student and practitioner in further exploring this field. You may like to move quickly through this part at first if you feel it is difficult to understand.

If Jia represents the subject of the astrology chart or Yijing prediction, a balanced Jia Wood person will have a healthy gallbladder system and strong life energy. Excess Jia indicates that the person will be susceptible to thyroid problems, inflammation in the gallbladder, or migraine headaches. Deficient Jia suggests the person will tend towards weakness in gallbladder function, gallstones, inadequate immune system response, neurological problems, or ankle pain.

Also, as a general reminder, whenever you are working to balance an Element in your clinical practice, please remember to consider the influence of the Yang and Yin organ pair correlations.

Numerology: 3

As discussed earlier, in the Daoist Five Elements numerological system, numbers themselves have Yin or Yang qualities. Even numbers have Yin quality energy whereas odd numbers are energetically more Yang. Three is the energy of Jia and itself is used as a medicine to balance Yang Wood or to strengthen life energy.

Alchemical Transformation: Earth

This information is commonly applied in Chinese cosmology, astrology, and Chinese medicine. In Chinese cosmology, Jia indicates a pattern of excess Earth, suggesting the associated weather patterns will have increased rain and dampness. With respect to Chinese astrology, Jia and Ji (the Heavenly Stem representing Yin Earth) transform to Earth energy when there is already strong Earth energy within the chart. In Chinese medicine, this

---

1 Wu, Master Zhongxian (2009) *Seeking the Spirit of The Book of Change: 8 Days to Mastering a Shamanic Yijing (I Ching) Prediction System.* London: Singing Dragon.

transformation principle allows another consideration when seeking to bring harmony to the dynamic between the gallbladder and spleen. We will continue to discuss the Chinese medicine applications of the transformation principles throughout the rest of this book.

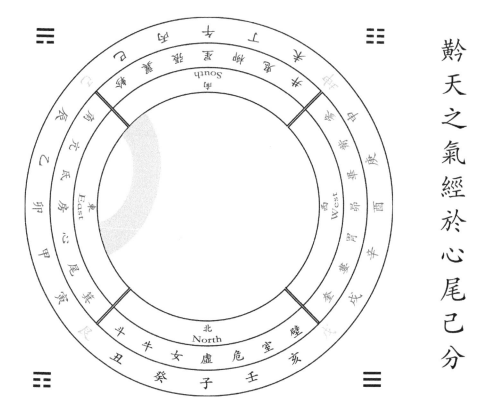

JinTianZhiQiJingYuXinWeiJiFen

黅天之氣經於心尾己分

The Yellow Heavenly Qi passes between [Lunar Mansions] *XinWei* and *Ji*

—*HuangDiNeiJing*, chapter 67

Figure 25: JiaJi Alchemical Transformation Diagram

Quality: Initiating, creative, straight, power, authority, ambition, anger, timid, powerless

The energetic qualities of the Stems are captured by specific attributes that help inform you during a Chinese astrology reading, a Yijing diagnosis, an acupuncture treatment, or a martial arts technique. They exist on a continuum of relative balance and imbalance. This principle applies to the rest of the Heavenly Stems, so we will rely on your own ability to remember the message of this commentary throughout the remainder of Chapter 2.

Internal Alchemy: The GanZhi Standing Posture

When we practice the standing posture of the GanZhi, we visualize ourselves connecting with the over-3000-year-old shaman-king bronze sculpture that was unearthed from *SanXingDui* site from which the Bronze Magic Tree of GanZhi was discovered (see Section 1.3). The bronze statue stands 1.82m (5.97ft) tall on top of a 0.8m (2.6ft) base, and weighs 180kg (397lbs). Please visualize this bronze shaman-king's powerful stance as shown in Figure 26 before you start your GanZhi internal alchemy practices for each Heavenly Stem and Earthly Branch. These practices will help you embody some of the symbolic meanings of the Stems and Branches, learning them more deeply through your own direct experience and felt sense.

Stand with your feet parallel, shoulder-width apart and toes grabbing the earth. Straighten your back so it is as solid as a mountain. Lift your perineum, sealing the *Dihu* 地户—Earthly Door (acupuncture point CV1). Tuck your lower abdomen in slightly. Open your chest. Keep your head upright. Open your *Tianmen* 天門 Heavenly Gate (acupuncture point GV20) and imagine your head is touching Heaven. Place the tip of your tongue on the tooth ridge behind your upper teeth. Keep your teeth and mouth closed. With shoulders down, arms relaxed, and armpits slightly open, let your hands hang comfortably by your sides with palms open and fingers straight. Relax your eyelids and bring your eyesight within. Listen within. With each breath, imagine breathing through your nose and through all the pores of your skin. Adjust your breathing to be slow, smooth, deep, and even. There should be no noise from your breathing. In Chinese, this breathing technique is called *MiMi MianMian* 密密綿綿—the breathing is soft and unbroken like a silk thread.

Please note: As this will be the same standing posture we will use for the internal alchemy practice for each subsequent GanZhi symbol, we will not repeat the instructions again. Instead, we will introduce the various visualization methods for each individual Stem and Branch.

Figure 26: Shang Dynasty bronze GanZhi standing meditation sculpture

Jia Internal Alchemy Practice: Facing east in the GanZhi standing posture, imagine green color Qi is entering into your gallbladder with each inhalation. With each exhalation, intensify your visualization: imagine your toes are grabbing the earth with more force, close your Earthly Door tighter, reach your fingertips deeper into the earth, and stretch your head taller to reach high into the heavens, all the while paying attention to your gallbladder. Repeat for a minimum of 49 breaths.

2.2 Yi 乙

Yi is the second Heavenly Stem and is the symbol for the number two or the second position. The ancient Chinese dictionary, *ShuoWenJieZi* 說文解字, defines Yi as a winding, growing plant—the character itself depicts this image. In old Chinese, Yi also is used to express twisting or fish guts.

The Oracle Script is associated with the Lunar Mansion *Kang* 亢 of the eastern sky. *Kang*, which means high, comprises four stars and forms the neck of the Green Dragon. When we draw a twisting line through these four stars we see the pattern of the Oracle Script for Yi.

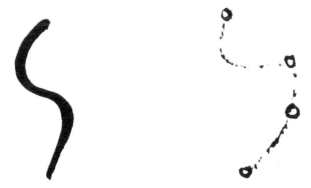

Figure 27: Star pattern—the source of the 乙 character

Element: YinMu 陰木 Yin Wood

Yin Wood (Yi) embodies flexibility with strength and compassion.

Spiritual Animal: *QingLong* 青龍 Green Dragon

Yi has the same spiritual animal as Jia—the Green Dragon.

Season: *ZhongChun* 仲春 Middle Spring

Yi is associated with the spring season, especially between March and April, the morning hours, as well as the

Figure 28: Green Dragon jade sculpture from HongShan 紅山 culture (circa 4700–2900 BCE)

period of strong, supple, and full of life "adolescent" energy of a person, animal, or plant.

Direction: *Dong* 東 East

Similar to Jia, "East" does not simply refer to the physical eastern direction, and can also be interpreted as the spiritual direction—the left side of your body or house, etc.

Trigram: ☴ *Xun* 巽 Wind

The trigram *Xun* is made with two Yang lines over one Yin line. This is the expression of spreading or penetrating Yang (life energy). Wind, which can seem deceptively gentle, also has a strong spreading and penetrating quality. Depending on the specific circumstance, Yi (Yin Wood) can bring either harmonious (cool relief on a hot, muggy day) or disastrous (spreading an uncontrollable wildfire or a devastating hurricane) effects to the natural world, to your relationships, or to your health. *Xun* also has many other symbolic meanings, some of which include older daughter, romance, monk, thigh, bird, and artwork.

Body: Liver, neck, immune system, tendons, ligaments, wrist, finger

If Yi represents the subject of the astrology chart or Yijing prediction, a balanced Yi Wood person usually has strong life energy and good health. If Yi is in excess, the person will likely have problems with neck stiffness, tight ligaments, or even hepatitis. If Yi is deficient, the person may have decreased immune function and be prone to develop arthritis or struggle with depression.

Numerology: 8

The number eight is used to represent Yin Wood energy—Yi—and itself can be used as treatment accordingly.

Alchemical Transformation: Metal

In Chinese cosmology, Yi transforms to deficient Metal, which increases the likelihood of windstorms and may also lead to outbreaks of the flu. With respect to Chinese astrology, Yi Wood will transform to Metal energy when Geng 庚 Metal is close by and the chart has other strong Metal Elements. In your clinical practice, keep in mind the dynamics between the liver and the large intestine when you make your diagnosis and develop a treatment plan.

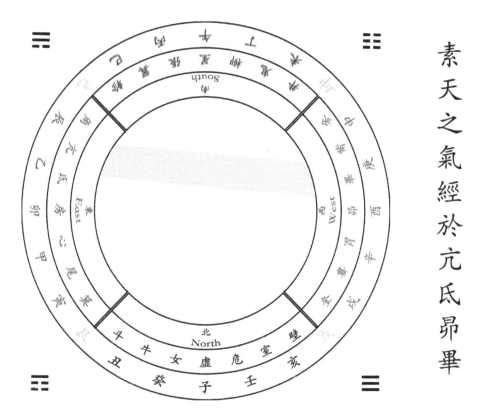

SuTianZhiQiJingYuKangDiMaoBi
素天之氣經於亢氐昴畢
The Pure Heavenly Qi passes between [Lunar Mansions] *KangDi* and *MaoBi*
—*HuangDiNeiJing*, chapter 67

Figure 29: YiGeng Alchemical Transformation Diagram

Quality: Flexible, gentle, compassionate, kindness, strength, vitality, depression, stiffness, temper, rage

Yi Internal Alchemy Practice: Facing east in the GanZhi standing posture, visualize green color Qi surrounding you and entering into your liver with each inhale. With each exhalation, intensify your visualization: imagine your toes are grabbing the earth with more force, close your Earthly Door tighter, reach your fingertips deeper into the earth, and stretch your head taller to reach high into the heavens, all the while paying attention to your liver. Repeat for a minimum of 49 breaths.

2.3 Bing 丙

Bing is the third Stem. As with the other Stems, Bing is commonly used when referring to the number three or the third position. It also symbolizes fire, clarity, or brightness. In ancient Chinese, it meant fishtail. You can see here that the old written character for Bing resembles a fishtail.

The Oracle Script for Bing is the image of the Lunar Mansion *Zhen* 軫, which lies in the domain of the southern Red Bird. Within the four stars of the *Zhen* pattern is a star named *ChangSha* 長沙. Once we can connect these five stars, the original pattern of Bing emerges.

 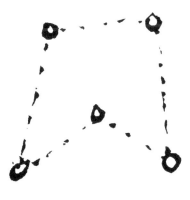

Figure 30: Star pattern—the source of the 丙 character

Element: YangHuo 陽火 Yang Fire

Yang Fire (Bing) is hot, bright, blazing, passionate, and exciting.

Spiritual Animal: *ZhuQue* 朱雀 Red Bird

Red is the color of the Qi from the southern direction. The bird is a symbol for freedom and uplifting energy. The Red Bird is the totem of ancient Chinese tribes from the south, and represents the southern sky. It is

Figure 31: Paper rubbing of the Red Bird from a Han Dynasty era stone carving

also the image of the seven southern Lunar Mansions. In terms of spiritual cultivation, it encapsulates the energy of spirit and enlightenment.

Season: *MengXia* 孟夏 Early Summer

Bing represents early summer (around the time of May–early June and late morning). According to Daoism and Chinese medicine, one 24-hour period also has four seasons, and Bing is the early summer period of a day: 09:00–10:59. It can be used to refer to any time or place that has the energetic quality of early summer.

Direction: *Nan* 南 South

Bing can be used to express the physical directions of south or southeast, as well as the energetic southern direction and "the front of"—for example, the front of yourself or of your house.

Trigram: ☲ *Li* 離 Fire

The trigram *Li* is composed of two Yang lines embracing a center Yin line. This is the image of an object with a hard outer layer that is soft on the inside, much like a crab, shellfish, or turtle. It is also the symbol for fire, bright, armor, middle daughter, joy, excitement, pheasant, and eyesight, among others.

Body: Small intestine, shoulder, forehead, eyesight

If Bing represents the subject of the astrology chart or Yijing prediction, a balanced Bing Fire person generally experiences good digestion and a state of overall good health. Excess Bing Fire, however, will influence a potential for inflammation in small intestine, shoulder pain, high blood pressure, or frontal headaches. With deficient Bing Fire comes weakness in digestive function or poor eyesight.

Numerology: 7

The Yang Fire number is 7 and it can be used to help strengthen the heart, small intestine, and the other body parts mentioned above.

Alchemical Transformation: Water

In Chinese cosmology, Bing Fire transforms to excess Water, which is an indication for heavy rain or snowstorms. In Chinese astrology, Bing Fire changes to Water when flanked by Yin Metal Stem Xin 辛 *and* when there are strong Water Elements present within the chart. This exemplifies a fundamental principle of Chinese astrology, cosmology, medicine, music, internal arts, and of life itself—*YinJiYangShengYangJiYinSheng* 陰極陽生陽極陰生—extremely Yin transforms to Yang, extremely Yang transforms to Yin.

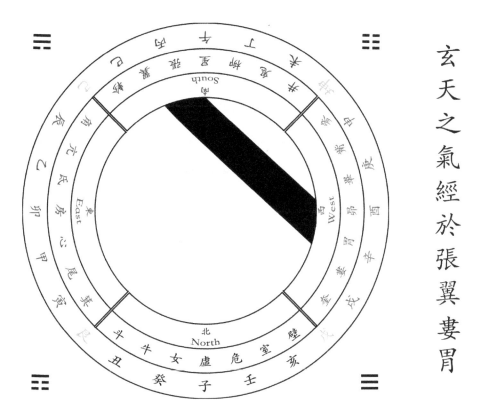

XuanTianZhiQiJingYuZhangYiLouWei

玄天之氣經於張翼婁胃

The Mystical Heavenly Qi passes between [Lunar Mansions] *ZhangYi* and *LouWei*
—*HuangDiNeiJing*, chapter 67

Figure 32: BingXin Alchemical Transformation Diagram

Quality: Exciting, thrilling, stimulating, vivacious, internal, quiet, over-stimulated

Bing Internal Alchemy Practice: Facing south in the GanZhi standing posture, visualize red color Qi surrounding you and entering into your small intestine with each inhalation. With each exhalation, intensify your visualization: imagine your toes are grabbing the earth with more force, close your Earthly Door tighter, reach your fingertips deeper into the earth, and stretch your head taller to reach high into the heavens, all the while paying attention to your small intestine. Repeat for a minimum of 49 breaths.

2.4 Ding 丁

Ding is the fourth Stem. It means nail, small, population, and fourth. As its written image suggests, it is also used in reference to anything that resembles a T-shape. The Oracle Script for Ding looks like a square, which suggests it originated in the *Gui* 鬼 Lunar Mansion of the southern sky. *Gui* means ghost or the returning place of spirits. It has four stars that when joined together form the pattern we recognize as Ding.

 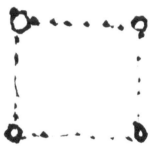

Figure 33: Star pattern—the source of the 丁 character

Element: YinHuo 陰火 Yin Fire

Yin Fire Ding has a different quality Fire than the burning intensity of Bing. It is more gentle, warm and loving.

Figure 34: Han Dynasty Red Bird wall painting from BuQianQiu 卜千秋 tomb in HeNan province

Spiritual Animal: *ZhuQue* 朱雀 Red Bird

As discussed in Section 2.3 Bing, red is the color of the Qi from the southern direction and the bird is a symbol for freedom and uplifting energy. The Red Bird was the totem of ancient Chinese tribes from the south. It represents the southern sky and is the image of the seven southern Lunar Mansions. In terms of spiritual cultivation, it encapsulates the energies of spirit and enlightenment.

Season: *ZhongXia* 仲夏 Middle Summer

Ding relates to the summer season, especially the months of June and July, the height of the afternoon, and the prime of life.

Direction: *Nan* 南 South

Again, this implies the physical/energetic south or the facing direction.

Trigram: ☲ *Li* 離 Fire

From the previous Heavenly Stem (Bing): The trigram *Li* is composed of two Yang lines embracing a center Yin line. This is the image of an object that is hard on the outside and soft on the inside, much like a crab, shellfish, or turtle. It is also the symbol for fire, bright, armor, middle daughter, joy, excitement, pheasant, and eyesight, among others.

Body: Heart, tongue, mouth

If Ding represents the subject of the astrology chart or Yijing prediction, a balanced Ding Fire person will experience fairly good health. Excess Ding Fire hints that the person may have problems with heart palpitations or a racing heart beat and may have chronic ulcers on the lips and/or inside the mouth. A deficient Ding Fire person is susceptible to a weak heart and poor blood circulation.

Numerology: 2

The number 2 is the numerological association of Yin Fire, and it is used to help strengthen the Fire Element of an environment or situation and all functions of the heart, and to help regulate blood pressure.

Alchemical Transformation: Wood

In Chinese cosmology, Ding Fire transforms to deficient Wood, bringing rain and damp conditions. In Chinese astrology, Ding will be converted to the Wood Element when it is in close association with Ren Yang Water, as long as the chart has other strong Wood Elements. Chinese medicine practitioners should remember to consider the relationship between the function of the heart and the liver/gallbladder when working with patients.

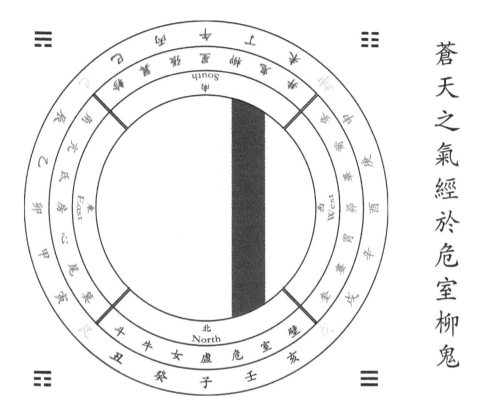

CangTianZhiQiJingYuWeiShiLiuGui

蒼天之氣經於危室柳鬼

The Green Heavenly Qi passes between [Lunar Mansions] *WeiShi* and *LiuGui*

—*HuangDiNeiJing*, chapter 67

Figure 35: DingRen Alchemical Transformation Diagram

Quality: Inspiring, passionate, adoring, warm, kind, benevolent, imaginative, delusional

Ding Internal Alchemy Practice: Facing south in the GanZhi standing posture, visualize red color Qi surrounding you and entering into your heart with each inhalation. With each exhalation, intensify your visualization: imagine your toes are grabbing the earth with more force, close your Earthly Door tighter, reach your fingertips deeper into the earth, and stretch your head taller to reach high into the heavens, all the while paying attention to your heart. Repeat for a minimum of 49 breaths.

2.5 Wu 戊

Wu 戊 is the fifth Stem. It means fifth and center. Originally, Wu 戊 held the meaning of lance or axe. The Oracle Script for Wu reminds us that it lies within the pattern of the stars of the central celestial realm, *ZiWei* 紫微. Nestled within *ZiWei* we find *GouChen* 勾陳, which is known as Ursa Minor (the Little Dipper) in the West. In Daoist mythology, *GouChen* is the Heavenly Emperor who rules the stars in the sky and the affairs of all beings on earth. We see the image of Wu 戊 by linking the stars of *GouChen* with neighboring stars.

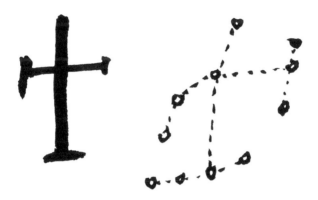

Figure 36: Star pattern—the source of the 戊 character

Figure 37: GouChen DaDi 勾陳大帝 Heavenly Emperor

Element: YangTu 陽土 Yang Earth

Yang Earth is condensed, dry and thick.

Spiritual Animal: *FengHuang* 鳳凰 Yellow Phoenix

Wu 戊 Earth does not have a fixed spiritual animal. The spirit of Wu 戊 is that of the *GouChen* (Ursa Minor) constellation. Yellow is the spiritual energetic color for the Earth stems Wu 戊 and Ji. In Daoist cultivation traditions, the Yellow Phoenix is the spiritual animal of Wu 戊. In internal alchemy practices, however, we recognize *HuangPo* 黃婆 (the Yellow Lady) as the spirit of Earth Element in its entirety. Within the Yijing prediction system, *GouChen* is known to be the spirit of Wu 戊.

Season: *SiJi* 四季 All seasons

Si means four and *Ji* means the third month of a season. *SiJi* means four seasons and it represents all seasons. The Earth Element is active during all seasons. The strongest times of annual cycle for Yang Earth Wu 戊 energy are the majority of the months of April and October. In the daily cycle, Wu 戊 energy predominates during the hours of 07:00–08:59 and 19:00–20:59.

Figure 38: Paper rubbing of Yellow Phoenix from a Han Dynasty era stone carving

Direction: Center

This can refer to the center of any object. During your inner cultivation practice or Yijing consultation, it represents your own self or your own location.

Trigram: ☶ *Gen* 艮 Mountain

Gen holds one Yang line on top of two Yin lines, creating an image of an upside-down bowl and a feeling of stability. The trigram *Gen* symbolizes steady, constant, younger son, hand, back of the body, trail, dog, honest, and others.

Body: Stomach, rib cage, face

If Wu 戊 represents the subject of the astrology chart or Yijing prediction, a balanced Wu 戊 Earth suggests the person has a hearty appetite and clear, smooth skin. The picture of a person with excess or deficient Wu 戊 Earth may manifest in stomach issues or someone with skin rashes, especially on the face.

Numerology: 5

5 is the Yang Earth number and is used to improve stomach function and help balance the Earth Element in general.

Alchemical Transformation: Fire

Within Chinese cosmology, Wu 戊 is known to transform into excess Fire and suggests the arrival of hot weather. In Chinese astrology, Wu 戊 transforms to Fire only when there is a Yin Water Stem (Gui) neighboring it and the Fire Elements in the chart are strong. Chinese medicine practitioners should remember the special connection between the Fire and Earth organ systems when treating patients.

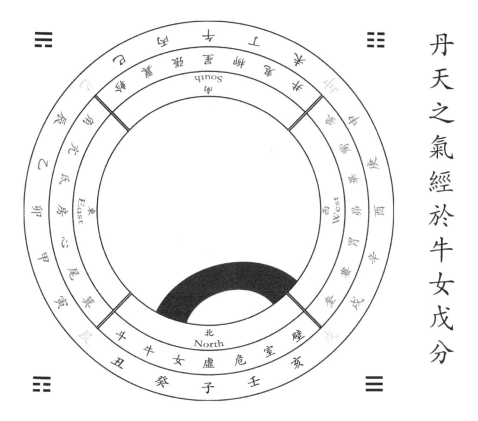

DanTianZhiQiJingYuNiuNüWuFen
丹天之氣經於牛女戊分
The Red Heavenly Qi passes between [Lunar Mansion] *NiuNü* and *Wu*
—*HuangDiNeiJing*, chapter 67

Figure 39: WuGui Alchemical Transformation Diagram

Quality: Stable, solid, centered, mature, stubborn, single-minded

Wu 戊 Internal Alchemy Practice: In the GanZhi standing posture, face northeast and visualize yellow color Qi surrounding you and entering into your stomach with each inhale. With each exhalation, intensify your visualization: imagine your toes are grabbing the earth with more force, close your Earthly Door tighter, reach your fingertips deeper into the earth, and stretch your head taller to reach high into the heavens, all the while paying attention to your stomach. Repeat for a minimum of 49 breaths.

2.6 Ji 己

Ji 己 is the sixth Stem and is used to represent the number six. The old meaning of Ji is a shape of twisted rope or silk threads. It commonly means self. The Oracle Script shows it is the shape of the Big Dipper. According to Daoist tradition, the Big Dipper is the center of the celestial world and the heart of the universe—it is the chariot of the Heavenly Emperor and the symbol that represents the Dao itself.

Figure 40: Star pattern—the source of the 己 character

Element: YinTu 陰土 Yin Earth

Different from dry Yang Earth Wu 戊, Ji Yin Earth is moist and damp. Its qualities are centered, nurturing, humble, and faithful.

Spiritual Animal: *FengHuang* 鳳凰 Yellow Phoenix

Similar to Wu 戊, Ji Earth does not have a fixed spiritual animal. The spirit of Ji is the Big Dipper of the central celestial region. In spiritual cultivation practice, the Yellow Phoenix is Ji's spiritual animal, and in internal

Figure 41: Han Dynasty Double Phoenix brick— excavated in ShaanXi 陝西 province

alchemy practices *HuangPo* 黃婆 (Yellow Lady) is the spirit of the Earth Element. Within the Yijing prediction systems, *TengShe* 騰蛇, the Flying Snake, is the spiritual animal of Ji.

Season: *SiJi* 四季 All seasons

Similar to Wu 戊, Ji is active in each season. The strongest time of Yin Earth Ji energy in the annual cycle are the months of Ox (around January) and Goat (most of July), and in the daily cycle between 01:00–02:59 and 13:00–14:59.

Direction: Center

As with Wu 戊, this can refer to the center of any object. During your inner cultivation practice or Yijing consultation, it represents your own self or your own location.

Trigram: ☷ *Kun* 坤 Earth

The trigram *Kun* contains three Yin lines and generates a feeling of openness and flow. *Kun* is also the symbol for earth, mother, cow, belly, square, and stability.

Body: Spleen, pancreas, belly, nose, flesh

If Ji represents the subject of the astrological chart or Yijing prediction and is balanced, it suggests that the person in general has good health and a rich life. Excess Ji Earth will manifest as an overweight body shape, big belly, a fullness or bloated sensation, and a susceptibility to diabetes. A person with deficient Ji will have spleen Qi deficiency symptoms, may have weak digestive function, or could be troubled with regular diarrhea.

Numerology: 10

10 is the Yin Earth number and is used to strengthen spleen Qi and digestive function.

Alchemical Transformation: Earth

Among all ten Stems, Ji is one of the two Stems that does not change its Five Elements character in alchemical transformation. In Chinese cosmology, Ji will transform to deficient Earth, indicating that the weather will bring heavy rain, snowstorms, or deep cold. In Chinese astrology, Ji can make Jia Wood transform to the Earth Element.

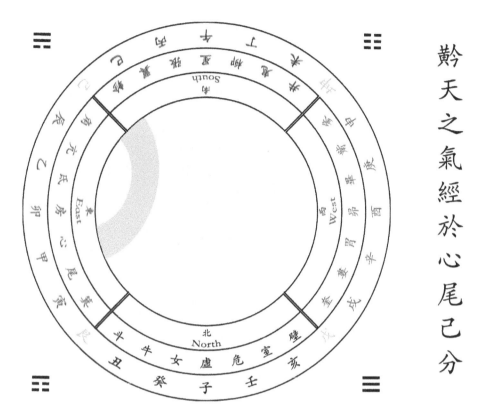

黅天之氣經於心尾己分

JinTianZhiQiJingYuXinWeiJiFen

黅天之氣經於心尾己分

The Yellow Heavenly Qi passes between *XinWei* (Lunar Mansion) and *Ji*

—*HuangDiNeiJing*, chapter 67

Figure 42: JiaJi Alchemical Transformation Diagram

Quality: Remarkable, humble, firm, faithful, thinker, heavy, doubtable, doubtful, peaceful, stable, virtuous, trustworthy, heavy (emotionally), worrisome, worried

Ji Internal Alchemy Practice: In the GanZhi standing posture, face southwest and visualize yellow color Qi surrounding you and entering into your spleen and pancreas with each inhalation. With each exhalation, intensify your visualization: imagine your toes are grabbing the earth with more force, close your Earthly Door tighter, reach your fingertips deeper into the earth, and stretch your head taller to reach high into the heavens, all the while paying attention to your spleen and pancreas. Repeat for a minimum of 49 breaths.

2.7 Geng 庚

Geng is the seventh Stem. It signifies seven, alternate, change, compensate, a person's age, and the name of the evening Venus (the morning and evening Venus are two of the many Chinese names for Venus). The Oracle Script for Geng is related to the Lunar Mansion *Shen* 參, which is found in the western celestial realm. *Shen* has seven stars and is known in the West as the constellation Orion. *Fa* 伐, a constellation that contains three stars, is found within *Shen*. When we link the ten stars of *Shen* and *Fa* together, we create the pattern of Geng.

Figure 43: Star pattern—the source of the 庚 *character*

Element: YangJin 陽金 Yang Metal

Yang Metal Geng is dry, sharp, powerful, sensitive, just, detached, cut off, judgmental, and aggressive.

Spiritual Animal: *BaiHu* 白虎 White Tiger

White means both clear and pure; it is the color of the west and of the Metal Element. Tiger represents descending energy and the vital

Figure 44: Paper rubbing of the White Tiger from a Han Dynasty era stone carving

breath of nature. White Tiger is the totem of ancient tribes in the west of China. It is also the pattern of the western seven Lunar Mansions. In inner cultivation practices, White Tiger symbolizes descending Qi and the clarity of awakened consciousness.

Season: *MengQiu* 孟穐 Early Autumn

In the annual cycle, the early autumn season occurs during August and September. This energy is also present in the afternoon and the middle-aged stage of life.

Direction: *Xi* 西 West

This can be interpreted physically or spiritually as the western or southwestern direction, or as the right side or front-right of your home or your body.

Trigram: ☰ *Qian* 乾 Heaven

Qian has three solid Yang lines and symbolizes the unbroken cycle of nature and the universal way. Other symbolic meanings for the trigram *Qian* include sky, heaven, father, a wise person, a round shaped object, horse, and head.

Body: Large intestine, navel, bones, skin

If the self is represented in the astrological chart or Yijing prediction as a balanced Geng, the person can expect to have healthy large intestine and circulatory system function. Excess Geng Metal may manifest as constipation, dry skin, or weakness of the immune system. Deficient Yang Metal Geng may reveal itself through poor Qi circulation and problems in large intestines, bones, or skin.

Numerology: 9

The Yang Metal number is 9, and it is used for improving Qi circulation, life energy, and immune system function.

Alchemical Transformation: Metal

With respect to Chinese cosmology, Geng will transform into excess Metal energy, which indicates the climate will be very dry and without rain. According to Chinese astrology principles, Geng Yang Metal will transform with Yi Yin Wood to form a Metal family. Chinese medicine practitioners should consider the interconnectedness of Metal and Wood in their clinical practice.

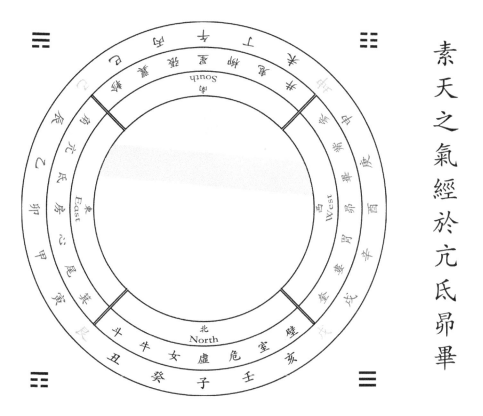

SuTianZhiQiJingYuKangDiMaoBi
素天之氣經於亢氐昴畢

The Pure Heavenly Qi passes between [Lunar Mansion] *KangDi* and *MaoBi*
—*HuangDiNeiJing*, chapter 67

Figure 45: YiGeng Alchemical Transformation Diagram

Quality: Sharp, just, righteous, clear, spiritual, good judgment, critical, judgmental, depressed, violent, misanthropy

Geng Internal Alchemy: In the GanZhi standing posture, face west and visualize white color Qi surrounding you and entering into your large intestine with each inhalation. With each exhalation, intensify your visualization: imagine your toes are grabbing the earth with more force, close your Earthly Door tighter, reach your fingertips deeper into the earth, and stretch your head taller to reach high into the heavens, all the while paying attention to your large intestine. Repeat for a minimum of 49 breaths.

2.8 Xin 辛

Xin is the eighth Stem. It means eighth, suffering, sad, aching, crime, and pungent. The Oracle Script character is a triangle, visible in the Lunar Mansions *Zi*, *Wei*, or *Lou*, which are located the western White Tiger celestial region.

Figure 46: Star pattern—the source of the 辛 character

Element: YinJin 陰金 Yin Metal

Xin Yin Metal is pure, clear, moist, righteous, and sensitive.

Figure 47: Shang Dynasty bronze White Tiger sculpture from SanXingDui 三星堆, SiChuan province

Spiritual Animal: *BaiHu* 白虎 White Tiger

As discussed previously, White means both clear and pure and is the color of the western direction and the Metal Element. The Tiger represents the vital breath of nature and descending energy. The White Tiger is the totem of ancient tribes in the west of China. It is also the pattern of the western seven Lunar Mansions. In inner cultivation practices, White Tiger symbolizes descending Qi and the clarity of awakened consciousness.

Season: *ZhongQiu* 仲穐 Middle Autumn

Xin resonates with the autumn season, especially with the months of September and October, the late afternoon and early evening, and the age of biological decline.

Direction: *Xi* 西 West

This can be interpreted spiritually or physically as the western direction, or the right side of your body or house.

Trigram: ☱ *Dui* 兑 Marsh, Lake

The trigram *Dui* has one Yin line above two Yang lines, and represents break, open, mouth, joy, negotiation, younger daughter, and goat.

Body: Lung, thigh, breath, Qi

If during a Chinese astrology or Yijing consultation the self is represented by a balanced Xin, the subject may have a keen sense of discipline and well-developed spiritual self. A person with imbalanced Xin Metal may have problems with lung function, breathing, Qi circulation, or immune function.

Numerology: 4

The Yin Metal number is 4, and it can be used to boost Qi and to nourish the lung.

Alchemical Transformation: Water

According to the principles of Chinese astrology, Xin Metal will transform to deficient Water, which suggests that the correlating climate pattern will be hot. In Chinese astrology, Xin transforms to Water when it is combined with Yang Fire Bing Stem and Water is already well represented in the chart.

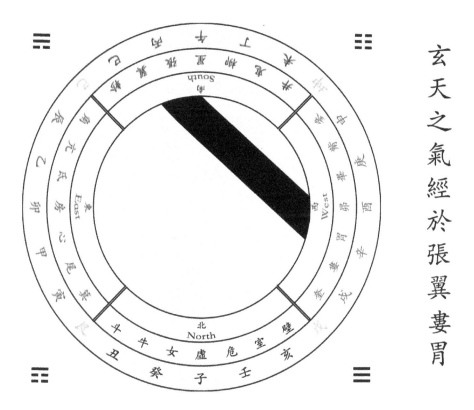

XuanTianZhiQiJingYuZhangYiLouWei
玄天之氣經於張翼婁胃

The Mystical Heavenly Qi passes between [Lunar Mansions] *ZhangYi* and *LouWei*
—*HuangDiNeiJing*, chapter 67

Figure 48: BingXin Alchemical Transformation Diagram

Quality: Sensitive, sympathetic, pure, communicative, miserable, offensive, overreacting, sad, unpleasant

Xin Internal Alchemy Practice: In the GanZhi standing posture, face west and visualize white color Qi surrounding you and entering into your lungs with each inhalation. With each exhalation, intensify your visualization: imagine your toes are grabbing the earth with more force, close your Earthly Door tighter, reach your fingertips deeper into the earth, and stretch your head taller to reach high into the heavens, all the while paying attention to your lungs. Repeat for a minimum of 49 breaths.

2.9 Ren 壬

Ren is the ninth Stem. In addition to meaning ninth, it is also the symbol for carry, burden, task, shin, nourish, conception, pregnant, and water. In Oracle Script, we can see that Ren is the pattern of the Lunar Mansion *Xü*, which is a part of the northern Mystical Warrior celestial realm. *Xü* has two stars; we draw a line linking these two stars to create the ideogram.

Figure 49: Star pattern—the source of the 壬 character

Element: YangShui 陽水 Yang Water

Ren is Yang Water. It is powerful and flowing.

Spiritual Animal: *XuanWu* 玄武 Mystical Warrior

Xuan means mystical, dark, unknown, and black, and is the color of northern Qi. *Wu* 武 means martial, weapon, and warrior. The spiritual animal *XuanWu* is a combination of a turtle and snake—*XuanWu* is commonly translated as Black Turtle-Snake. The turtle and snake symbolize the preserving quality of nature and of the life source, as well as the ability to store energy deep within.

Figure 50: Han Dynasty Mystical Warrior on clay brick, excavated in ShaanXi province

Season: *MengDong* 孟冬 Early Winter

In the annual cycle, early winter falls around the time period of the month of November and early December. It corresponds to the late evening and the stage of retirement.

Direction: *Bei* 北 North

North can represent the physical or spiritual north or northwest direction as well as the back side or right-back side of a person or object.

Trigram: ☵ *Kan* 坎 Water

The trigram *Kan* has one Yang line within two Yin lines. It is the image of Yang (power) hidden within Yin (softness). *Kan* is best represented by water. Water appears soft but is capable of overcoming hardness. We see this in nature quite often, for example, in granite riverbeds that are shaped smooth by flowing water. Other symbolic meanings of *Kan* include trap, hole, ear, middle daughter, pig, and wisdom.

Body: Urinary bladder, lower leg, ear

If during a Chinese astrology or Yijing consultation the self is represented as a balanced Ren Water, the person in question is likely to live a life blessed with good health. Excess or deficient Ren Water may manifest in urinary bladder problems, back pain, weak knees, or poor blood circulation.

Numerology: 1

The Yang Water number is 1. It is used to help enhance the function of the urinary bladder system.

Alchemical Transformation: Wood

With respect to Chinese cosmology, Ren Yang Water will transform to excess Wood, which brings with it a climate pattern where windstorms predominate. In Chinese astrology, Ren will be transformed to Wood when it is connected to the Yin Fire Stem Ding and the chart strong Wood Elements within. Chinese medicine practitioners should pay attention to the influencing factors among Water, Wood, and Fire.

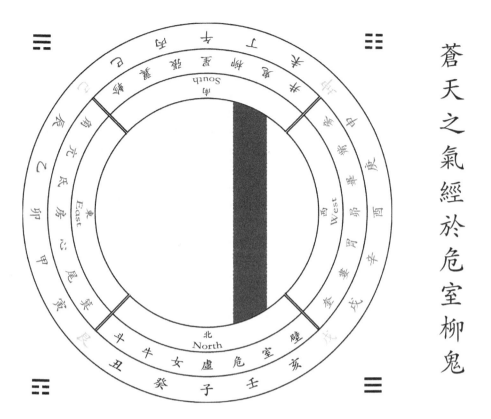

蒼天之氣經於危室柳鬼

CangTianZhiQiJingYuWeiShiLiuGui

蒼天之氣經於危室柳鬼

The Green Heavenly Qi passes between [Lunar Mansions] *WeiShi* and *LiuGui*

—*HuangDiNeiJing*, chapter 67

Figure 51: DingRen Alchemical Transformation Diagram

Quality: Flow, soft, smart, nourishing, easy, fear, overwhelm, devastation

Ren Internal Alchemy Practice: In the GanZhi standing posture, face north and visualize mystical Qi (like moon light or the northern lights) surrounding you and entering into your bladder with each inhalation. With each exhalation, intensify your visualization: imagine your toes are grabbing the earth with more force, close your Earthly Door tighter, reach your fingertips deeper into the earth, and stretch your head taller to reach high into the heavens, all the while paying attention to your bladder. Repeat for a minimum of 49 breaths.

2.10 Gui 癸

Gui is the last Stem. It embodies tenth, estimate, measure, and foot. The Oracle Script for Gui looks like two diagonal lines crossing each other. This pattern is easily derived from linking two Lunar Mansions *Bi* 壁 and *Shi* 室 of the northern *XuanWu* pattern. *Bi* and *Shi* are found next to each other, each containing two stars. Link the two crossing stars with oblique lines and see Gui in the stars.

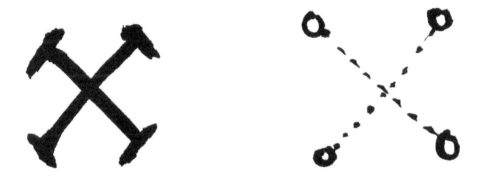

Figure 52: Star pattern—the source of the 癸 character

Element: YiShui 陰水 Yin Water

Among all the Heavenly Stems, Yin Water Gui is the paragon of Yin. It is very soft and gentle. However, as it is also true that extremely Yin will transform to Yang, the ultimate Yin Water Gui can transform to the Fire Element.

Spiritual Animal: *XuanWu* 玄武 Mystical Warrior

As discussed previously, *Xuan* means mystical, dark, unknown, and black, and is the color of northern Qi. *Wu* 武 means martial, weapon, and warrior. The spiritual animal *XuanWu* is a combination of a turtle and snake and is commonly translated as Black Turtle-Snake. The turtle and snake symbolize the preserving quality of nature and of the life source, as well as the ability to store energy deep within.

Season: *ZhongDong* 仲冬 Middle Winter

Winter energy is most apparent during the months of December and January. It is also encapsulated in the hours of the night and in old age.

Figure 53: Tang Dynasty Mystical Warrior wall painting

Direction: *Bei* 北 North

This represents the physical or spiritual northern direction or the back of an object, such as house or physical body.

Trigram: ☵ *Kan* 坎 Water

The trigram *Kan* represents Ren and Gui. It is the image of Yang (power) hidden within Yin (softness). *Kan* is best represented by water. Water appears soft but is capable of overcoming hardness. Other symbolic meanings of *Kan* include trap, hole, ear, middle daughter, pig, and wisdom.

Body: Kidney, foot, egg and sperm, blood, sexual energy, brain

If a balanced Gui represents the self or subject during an astrology or Yijing reading, it indicates a person with good genes, a sharp mind, and overt sexuality. Excess Gui manifests as a heaviness in the body, difficulties walking, and heart and/or blood problems. With deficient Gui you may see lower back pain, poor memory, and decreased libido.

Numerology: 6

The Yin Water number is 6 and it is used to help balance Yin Water Gui and strengthen kidney Qi.

Alchemical Transformation: Fire

In Chinese cosmology, Yin Water Gui transforms to deficient Fire, which indicates a dry weather pattern that weakens the function of the lung and heart. With respect to Chinese astrology, Gui transforms to Fire Element once it is paired with Yang Earth Wu 戊 and there are also strong Fire Elements in the chart. Chinese medicine practitioners should remember the interactions between Water, Fire, and Earth when working with patients.

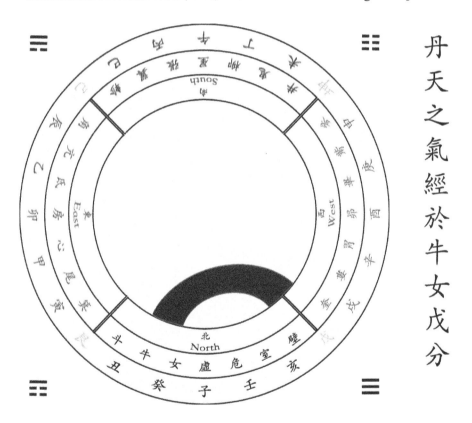

DanTianZhiQiJingYuNiuNüWuFen

丹天之氣經於牛女戊分

The Red Heavenly Qi passes between [Lunar Mansion] *NiuNü* and *Wu*

—*HuangDiNeiJing*, chapter 67

Figure 54: WuGui Alchemical Transformation Diagram

Quality: Wise, talented, artistic, easygoing, attractive, sexy, fearful, inward, easily shocked, poor social skills

Gui Internal Alchemy Practice: In the GanZhi standing posture, face north and visualize mystical Qi (like moon light or the northern lights) surrounding you and entering into your kidneys with each inhalation. With each exhalation, intensify your visualization: imagine your toes are grabbing the earth with more force, close your Earthly Door tighter, reach your fingertips deeper into the earth, and stretch your head taller to reach high into the heavens, all the while paying attention to your kidneys. Repeat for a minimum of 49 breaths.

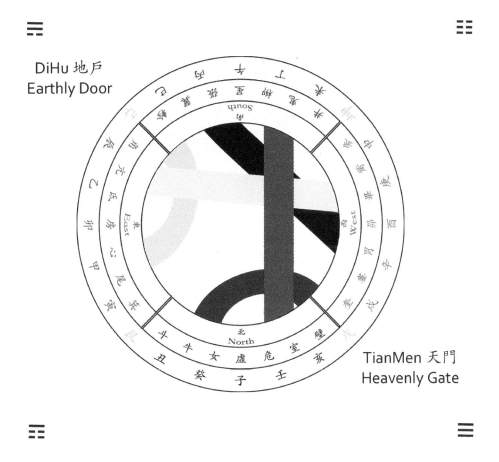

Figure 55: Heavenly Stems Transformation Diagram
As discussed in chapter 67 of the *HuangDiNeiJing*, the knowledge of the Heavenly Stems transformation principle comes directly from the cosmos, via the 28 Lunar Mansions and pathways of the Five Heavenly Qi as they cross the sky.

癸巳仲夏吉日
范之子 松瑞典

3

DiZhi XiangShu 地支象數

Earthly Branch Symbolism

We will now discuss the *XiangShu* (the symbolic and numerological meanings) of the twelve Earthly Branches. Earthly Branches are more complex than Heavenly Stems so we will include additional information for those at a higher level in their Chinese medicine or internal alchemy practice.

For example, each Earthly Branch has hidden Stems, called *RenYuan* 人元 (human source). *RenYuan* plays an important role in Chinese astrology and in internal alchemy practices. Traditionally, the twelve Branches represents the twelve seasonal Qi or natural energy patterns of the annual, monthly, daily, and hourly cycles. These twelve Qi are also traditionally described in *LüLü* 律呂—the twelve classical Chinese musical pitches. We have added information on *RenYuan* and *LüLü* in each Earthly Branch section.

Figure 56: Tang Dynasty twelve animal clay statues from ShaanXi province

An often-missed yet essential detail about Branches is that each Branch embodies one organ system and one meridian system. We will discuss the Five Element characteristics of these systems as they relate to each Branch in the "body" sections that follow. Conditions in which alchemical transformations occur between and among the Earthly Branches are more elaborate than those in the Heavenly Stems. Although we will outline the various alchemical relationships in Chapter 4, this specific information on alchemical transformation will make most sense for those who are already advanced practitioners.

3.1 Zi 子

Zi is the first Earthly Branch. It means baby, descendant, master, small, young, love, seed, and pit. The Oracle Script Zi is the replication of the pattern of Lunar Mansions *Xü* 虛 and *Wei* 危 of the northern Mystical Warrior celestial region of the night sky. Zi lies in the heart of the northern Mystical Warrior and *Kan* 坎 ☵ Water is its trigram.

Figure 57: Star pattern—the source of the 子 character

Element: Water

As discussed in Section 1.5, noting the Yin and Yang qualities of the Earthly Branches is much more complicated than noting the simple Yin or Yang characteristics of the Heavenly Stems. The Earthly Branches have three YinYang classification systems—each Branch may be classified as both Yin and Yang, depending on the context.

The physical body of Zi Water is Yang and its energetic function is Yin. This means that we are using Zi in the context of the Chinese calendar, its physical quality is Yang, and when we are using Zi in the context of an astrological chart or Chinese medicine, its energetic quality is Yin.

Spiritual Animal: Rat

Generally speaking, the spiritual animal of each Earthly Branch is derived from the spiritual animal of its associated Lunar Mansion.

Rat is the spiritual animal of the *Xü* Lunar Mansion in the central position of the northern Mystical Warrior celestial region. Rat symbolizes strong life energy, wisdom, and sexuality. For more details about the symbolic meaning of the twelve spiritual animals of the Earthly Branches, please read *The 12 Chinese Animals: Create Harmony in your Daily Life through Ancient Chinese Wisdom.*[1]

Figure 58: Rat painting by fifth Ming Dynasty emperor XuanDe 宣德 *(1431 CE)*

Season: December 7–January 5: *DaXue* 大雪 Major Snow and *DongZhi* 冬至 Winter Solstice

This is the middle month of the winter—the darkest period of the year in the northern hemisphere. Remember: extremely Yin gives birth to Yang. After the Yin energy has reached its peak, Yang energy is generated. This is

---

1   Wu, Master Zhongxian (2010) *The 12 Chinese Animals: Create Harmony in your Daily Life through Ancient Chinese Wisdom.* London: Singing Dragon.

the time to preserve your life energy and for rejuvenation. In an individual life cycle, it also encompasses the magical moment of conception and the prenatal existence inside the mother's womb.

Hour: 23:00–00:59

This is one of the best times of the day for deep meditation or sleep.

Direction: North

As before, the direction can imply the physical or spiritual direction, and can refer to the northern position, or the back of a house or your body.

Hexagram: ䷗ *Fu* 復 Rebirth

The trigram has one Yang line beneath five Yin lines, which signifies that new life energy is starting. It is also an image of thunder shaking the world.

Body: Kidney organ system, gallbladder meridian system

This section is specifically intended for seasoned Qigong and Chinese medicine practitioners. You may like to move through it more quickly if Chinese medicine is not your primary interest.

The kidney organ is of the Water Element. The gallbladder organ is of the Wood Element and the gallbladder meridian system is classified as *ShaoYang* 少陽, the Minor Yang, which is the Fire Element (specifically Ministerial Fire). According to Daoist internal alchemy traditions, Zi is the best time to enhance your kidney energy and restore your vitality—not only because the northern Mystical Warrior invigorates the kidney but also because *ShaoYang* Fire acts as thunder energizing kidney Water. It is always a good idea to provide added support to the gallbladder meridian system when working with someone who has a kidney condition—it will greatly enhance the therapeutic results and your clients will be very happy.

Numerology: 1 and 6

The Yang Water number is 1 and the Yin Water number is 6. Both are used to help balance Water Element.

Alchemical Transformation: *ShaoYin JunHuo* 少陰君火
Minor Yin Imperial Fire

In Chinese cosmology, Zi Water transforms to *ShaoYin* (Minor Yin Imperial Fire) energy, which means the climate pattern will heat up and will affect function of the kidney and heart. In the body, the Qi in the kidney meridian and heart meridian expresses this *ShaoYin* Fire energy.

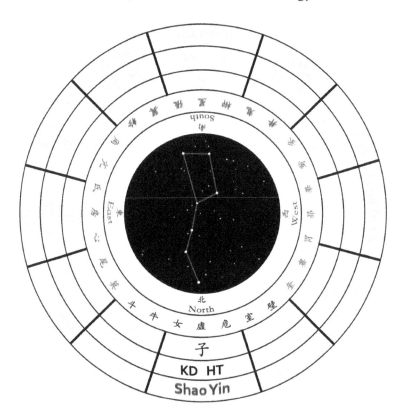

Zi transforms to *ShaoYin*, as expressed in the kidney and heart meridians.

Figure 59: Zi Alchemical Transformation Diagram

Quality: Wise, flexible, optimistic, honorable

If Zi is in your basic chart and well supported, you have the potential to be wise, flexible, optimistic, and honorable. If Zi is in your Destiny Palace, you are likely to have big heart, strong will, and to be very creative. However, if Zi represents excess or deficient Water in your chart it is more likely you will have foolish tendencies, a selfish attitude, carry strong fears, and/or can slip into wretchedness.

RenYuan 人元 **(Hidden Stem):** Gui 癸

Zi is in the northern cardinal direction and the winter season—it holds concentrated pure Yin Water Gui.

LüLü 律呂 **(Musical Pitch):** *HuangZhong* 黃鐘

In Daoist cultivation practices and Chinese medicine, we use *LüLü* to measure the rhythm of nature, the cyclical patterns of Qi and the meridian system in our bodies. *HuangZhong,* which literally means Yellow Bell, refers to an ancient Chinese bronze musical bell and is the fundamental scale of *LüLü.*

HuangZhong is strong Yang Qi from deep within the earth moving upward during the winter solstice. It is also the vibration of new life energy, which is associated with the gallbladder meridian system in the body. In the modern musical system, it is equal to tonic/unison or C.

Zi Internal Alchemy Practice: In the GanZhi standing posture, face north and visualize mystical Qi (like moon light or the northern lights) surrounding you and entering into your kidneys with each inhalation. With each exhalation, intensify your visualization: imagine your toes are grabbing the earth with more force, close your Earthly Door tighter, reach your fingertips deeper into the earth, and stretch your head taller to reach high into the heavens, all the while paying attention to your gallbladder meridian. Repeat for a minimum of 49 breaths.

3.2 Chou 丑

Chou is the second Branch. It means ugly, hateful, and twisted. The Oracle Script for Chou is shaped like a hand. It originates from the Lunar Mansions *Nü* 女 and *Niu* 牛 and its corresponding trigram is *Gen* 艮 ☶ Mountain.

Figure 60: Star pattern—the source of the 丑 character

Element: Earth

Both the physical and energetic qualities of Chou are Yin Earth.

Spiritual Animal: Ox

The Ox is the spiritual animal of the Lunar Mansion *Niu* 女 in the northern Mystical Warrior region of the celestial world, which is how it came to be the spiritual animal of Chou.

Season: January 6–February 4: *XiaoHan* 小寒 Minor Cold and *DaHan* 大寒 Major Cold

Figure 61: Shang Dynasty jade Ox sculpture

This time period represents the third and the final month of the winter season. It is the coldest time of a year, often the most challenging time, with hibernators in their deepest sleeping state and plants holding their life energy stored within their deepest roots. It signifies both maternity and birth.

Hour: 01.00–02.59 This is the time of day for deep rest.

Direction: Northeast

This can represent the physical or spiritual northeastern direction or back-left side of a building or your body.

Hexagram: ䷒ *Lin* 臨 Deliver

This tidal hexagram has four Yin lines on top of two Yang lines. It shows the Yang energy is stronger than in the previous stage *Fu* and is working hard to reach an equal state with Yin energy. The symbolic meaning of *Lin* is work hard, deliver, approach, and push.

Body: Spleen organ system, liver meridian system

The Spleen organ system is of the Earth Element. The liver organ is of the Wood Element and the liver meridian system is *JueYin* 厥陰 Reverse Yin Wind Wood. Like the trees of a forest, Wood needs Earth (e.g. soil) to be nourished, held, and rooted. Earth also needs Wood to bind it together and remain stable. The optimal functioning of spleen and liver are interdependent.

Numerology: 5 and 10

The Yin Earth number is 5 and the Yang Earth number is 10, and both are used traditionally to help support Earth's function.

Alchemical Transformation: *TaiYin ShiTu* 太陰濕土
Major Yin Damp Earth

In the Five Elements alchemical transformation system, Chou does not change its Earth quality. In Chinese cosmology, Chou transforms to Major Yin Damp Earth energy, which manifests as cloudy and rainy weather. This *TaiYin* energy is expressed in the body in both the spleen meridian system and lung meridian system.

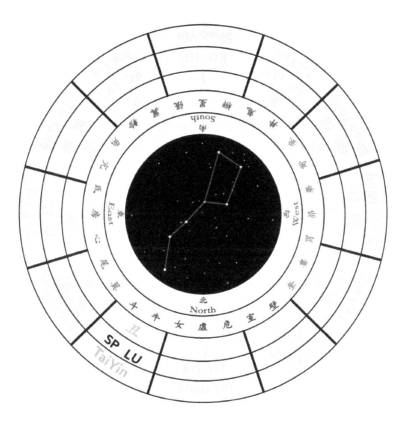

Chou transforms to *TaiYin*, as expressed in the spleen and lung meridians.

Figure 62: Chou Alchemical Transformation Diagram

Quality: Stable, kind, straight, endurance, tough, obstinate, hesitation

A balanced Chou Earth in the astrological chart suggests a character with stability, kindness, toughness, and firm qualities. When there is excess or deficient Earth, Chou may express a more challenging nature—unstable, hesitating, stubborn, and full of longing.

RenYuan 人元 **(Hidden Stem):** Ji 己, Xin 辛, Geng 癸

It is difficult to measure the energy of each hidden Stem. Some modern texts use percentages to describe the power of each hidden Stem within a Branch. For example, Chou has been said to be 70 percent Ji, 20 percent Xin, and 10 percent Gui. However, as life is not fixed but always changing, the force of each hidden Stem will change as circumstances change. Accordingly, we will not use percentages to discuss the energies of hidden

Stems in this book. Instead, we follow the traditional way and analyze the strength of each hidden Stem within its context.

Ji Earth is the main energy of the hidden Stems as Ji and Chou both belong to the Earth family. Chou is also the storage of the Metal Element and Xin Metal will show stronger energy when there are Metal Geng and/ or Xin Stems in the chart. Chou represents the last month of the Water season, so Gui will be strong once there is Ren and/or Gui Water in the chart.

LüLü 律呂 (Musical Pitch): *DaLü* 大呂

The vibration of *DaLü* supports the *HuangZhong* (the musical tone of the previous month's *LüLü* Qi) in its ascension, and continues to move Yang Qi upward in order to welcome the beginning of new life energy. The Qi of *DaLü* resonates through the liver meridian system. It is equal to the modern musical system semitone of D♭/C#.

Chou Internal Alchemy Practice: In the GanZhi standing posture, face northeast and visualize yellow color Qi surrounding you and entering into your spleen and pancreas with each inhalation. With each exhalation, intensify your visualization: imagine your toes are grabbing the earth with more force, close your Earthly Door tighter, reach your fingertips deeper into the earth, and stretch your head taller to reach high into the heavens, all the while paying attention to your liver meridian. Repeat for a minimum of 49 breaths.

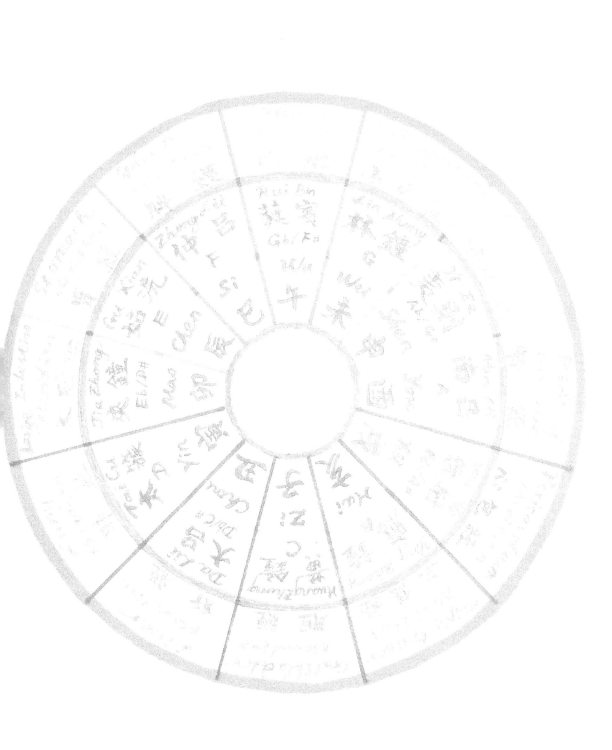

3.3 Yin 寅

Yin 寅 is the third Branch. It carries the meanings of respectful, sincere, and display. The Oracle Script for Yin looks like an arrow and is related to the Lunar Mansions *Ji* 箕 and *Wei* 尾 in the eastern Green Dragon celestial region. Yin 寅 is also associated with the trigram *Gen* 艮 ☶ Mountain.

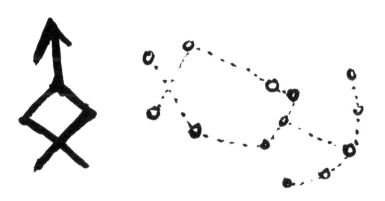

Figure 63: Star pattern—the source of the 寅 *character*

Element: Wood

From each perspective, Yin 寅 Wood has Yang qualities.

Spiritual Animal: Tiger

Tiger is the spiritual animal of the Lunar Mansion *Wei* in the eastern Green Dragon celestial region. Tiger represents power and authority. Please remember that this Tiger is *not* the same as the White Tiger of the four spiritual animals.

Figure 64: Zhou Dynasty jade Tiger ornament

Season: February 5–March 5: *LiChun* 立春 Establish Spring and *YuShui* 雨水 Rain Water

This is the first month of spring, when the strength of Yang energy throughout nature is ascending and the earth once again becomes peppered with buds, new growth, and early spring flowers. Yin 寅 symbolizes all new life or a baby state.

Hour: 03.00–04.59

With Yang energy on the rise, this is the time for cultivating life energy. In the Daoist tradition, the Yin 寅 hour is ideal for chanting, meditation, internal cultivation practices, and rigorous physical activity.

Direction: Northeast

This can represent the physical and spiritual northeastern direction as well as the left-back side of a building or yourself.

Hexagram: ䷊ *Tai* 泰 Balance

Hexagram *Tai* is made by three Yin lines on top of three Yang lines. This is the image of Yin and Yang energies as they have reached a totally balanced state.

Body: Gallbladder organ system, lung meridian system

The gallbladder organ system is of the Wood Element. The lung organ is of the Metal Element and the meridian system is *TaiYin*—Major Yin Damp Earth—an Earth Element classification. In some circumstances, Metal can control and cut off Wood. In others, Metal with a Damp Earth quality will support the Wood to grow. Sometimes proper functioning of the lung meridian is also dependent on healthy gallbladder function—Wood can act to hold Earth (*TaiYin*) stable.

Numerology: 3 and 8

The Yang Wood number is 3 and the Yin Wood number is 8. Both are used to support Wood function.

Alchemical Transformation: *ShaoYang XiangHuo* 少陽相火
Minor Yang Ministerial Fire

In Chinese cosmology, Yin 寅 Wood transforms to *ShaoYang*, the Minor Yang Ministerial Fire which indicates that the weather will be dominated by heat. In the body, *ShaoYang* Fire corresponds with the gallbladder meridian and the triple burner meridian.

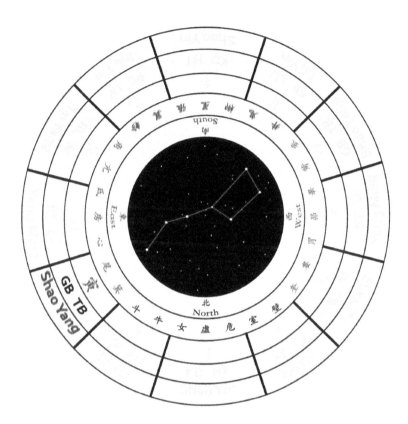

Yin transforms to *ShaoYang*, as expressed in the gallbladder and triple burner meridians.

Figure 65: Yin Alchemical Transformation Diagram

Quality: Careful, responsible, moral, power, graceful, friendly, anger, haughty

In terms of Chinese astrology, a healthy Yin 寅 Wood person is likely to be careful, responsible, moral, powerful, graceful, and friendly, with a tendency towards irascibility and arrogance. If Yin 寅 is a part of the Destiny Palace, the person is likely to be someone who comes to power easily and has strong leadership skills.

RenYuan 人元 **(Hidden Stem):** Jia 甲, Wu 戊, Bing 丙

The Yang Stem Jia Wood is the predominate influence of the hidden Stems. Wu 戊 Earth will be more powerful if Wu 戊 and/or Ji 己 appear elsewhere in the chart. Bing will have more of an impact if Bing 丙, Ding 丁, and/or Wu 午 are also present.

LüLü 律吕 (**Musical Pitch**): *TaiCu* 太簇

This frequency represents the strengthening of Yang Qi as it reaches a YinYang balance state. The strong Yang Qi vibration is like a cluster of arrows, cocked and ready to shoot. In our body, *TaiCu* represents our lung meridian Qi. It is equal to the modern musical pitch major second or D.

Yin Internal Alchemy Practice: In the GanZhi standing posture, face northeast and visualize green color Qi surrounding you and entering into your gallbladder with each inhalation. With each exhalation, intensify your visualization: imagine your toes are grabbing the earth with more force, close your Earthly Door tighter, reach your fingertips deeper into the earth, and stretch your head taller to reach high into the heavens, all the while paying attention to your lung meridian. Repeat for a minimum of 49 breaths.

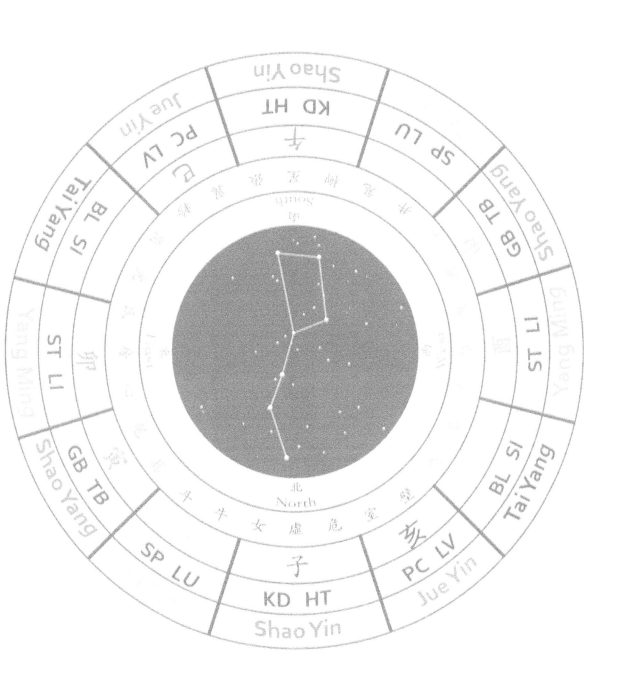

3.4 Mao 卯

Mao is the fourth Branch. It means roll call, mortise, prosper, or come out. The Oracle Script for Mao looks like an opening gate, which represents the earth opening its door to allow everything to grow. The shape is related to the *Xin* 心 and *Fang* 房 Lunar Mansions in the eastern Green Dragon celestial region. Its trigram is *Zhen* 震 ☳ Thunder.

Figure 66: Star pattern—the source of the 卯 character

Element: Wood

Both the body and function of Mao is Yin Wood.

Spiritual Animal: Rabbit

The Rabbit is originally the spiritual animal of the Lunar Mansion Fang 房. It is the symbol for smart, prosperity, and vitality.

Season: March 6–April 5: *JingZhe* 驚蟄 Awaken Hibernators and *ChunFen* 春分 Vernal Equinox

This is the time that nature blossoms and prospers. It also is used to describe the teenage years or any energy that is bursting with life.

Figure 67: Rabbit painting by CuiBai 崔白 (circa 1050–1080 CE)

Hour: 05.00–06.59

This time period is also one of the best times for your Qigong or other internal cultivation practice.

Direction: East

Mao is used to represent the spiritual or physical eastern direction. It can also be something on the left side of your house or your body.

Hexagram: ䷡ *DaZhuang* 大壯 Prosper

This hexagram has four Yang lines beneath two Yin lines. From the previous hexagram *Tai*, this depicts the Yang energy continuing to advance, symbolizing great strength of an object or your body.

Body: Liver organ system, large intestine meridian system

The Liver organ system is of the Yin Wood Element. Both the large intestine organ and meridian systems are of the Yang Metal Element. Together, Yin Wood and Yang Metal can transform to the Metal family. As such, working with both the liver and large intestine systems simultaneously will help improve the Qi circulation and the function of the immune system.

Numerology: 3 and 8

These are the same as the previous Branch Yin 寅 Tiger. Both 3 (Yin number) and 8 (Yang number) are used to help balance the Wood Element.

Alchemical Transformation: *YangMing ZaoJin* 陽明燥金
Yang Brightness Dry Metal

In Chinese cosmology, Mao will transform to *YangMing* (Yang Brightness Dry Metal), which has a Yang Metal quality. This indicates that the climate pattern will be dry. In the human body, *YangMing* Dry Metal manifests in the stomach and large intestine meridians.

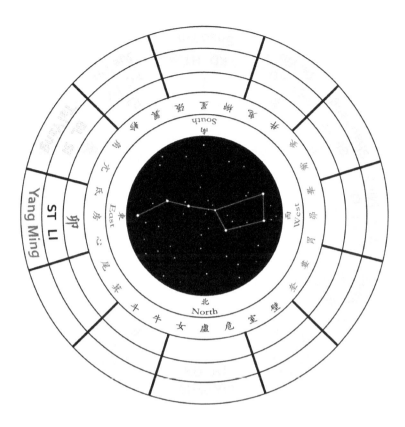

Yin transforms to *YangMing*, as expressed in the stomach and large intestine meridians.

Figure 68: Mao Alchemical Transformation Diagram

Quality: Clever, intelligent, agile, compassionate, strength, kind, rage, temper

In Chinese astrology, a balanced and well-supported Mao person may exhibit clever, intelligent, agile, compassionate, strong, and kind qualities. Mao in a chart that is either excess or deficient Wood may manifest as strong tempered or even full of rage. If Mao is in the Destiny Palace of the chart, the person will likely move through life guided by high moral standards.

RenYuan 人元 **(Hidden Stem):** Yi 乙

Yi is in the cardinal eastern position and the middle of the spring season. Therefore, it holds pure and condensed Yin Wood energy.

LüLü 律呂 (Musical Pitch): *JiaZhong* 夾鐘

The vibration of *JiaZhong* acts to spreads Yang Qi or life energy everywhere. In the body, it manifests as the Qi of the large intestine meridian system. It is equal to the modern musical scale minor third or E♭/D#.

Mao Internal Alchemy Practice: In the GanZhi standing posture, face east and visualize green color Qi surrounding you and entering into your liver with each inhale. With each exhalation, intensify your visualization: imagine your toes are grabbing the earth with more force, close your Earthly Door tighter, reach your fingertips deeper into the earth, and stretch your head taller to reach high into the heavens, all the while paying attention to your large intestine meridian. Repeat for a minimum of 49 breaths.

圖化行五氏吳

3.5 Chen 辰

Chen is the fifth Branch. The character itself means shake, beautiful, or nice looking. It is also the name of the Polar Star, Mercury, and an ancient Chinese city known for producing the best quality cinnabar. The Branch Chen is associated with the Lunar Mansions *Jiao* 角 and *Kang* 亢 in the eastern Green Dragon celestial region, the image of which can be seen replicated in the Oracle Script. The trigram of Chen is *Xun* 巽 ☴ Wind.

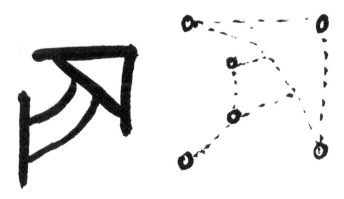

Figure 69: Star pattern—the source of the 辰 *character*

Element: Earth

Chen is a Yang Branch with a Yang Earth quality.

Spiritual Animal: Dragon

The spiritual animal of Chen comes from the *Kang* Lunar Mansion in eastern Green Dragon celestial region. Dragon is a symbol for rising Yang Qi and great transformation.

Season: April 5–May 6: *QingMing* 清明 Pure Brightness and *GuYu* 谷雨 Grain Rain

This is the time to clear the weeds from your garden and fields in order to make space for your plants to be healthy and grow. It is also the time period when a person transitions from a teen to young adult, as well as any time of great transformation in life.

Hour: 07.00–08.59

This is the best time to have your first and most substantial meal of the day.

Figure 70: In 1987, dragon and tiger images made of clamshells were discovered in a tomb from the Xishuipo 西水坡 Yangshao 仰韶 Culture Site in Puyang 濮陽 city (HeNan 河南 province). The tomb occupant was clearly a man of special status. On the right of his skeleton lies a 1.7m (5.6ft) dragon, and on the left, a 1.39m (4.6ft) tiger. This dragon is one of the earliest dragon images discovered in China—it is about 6500 years old.

Direction: Southeast

This indicates either the spiritual and physical southeast direction as well as the left-front side of a house or your body.

Hexagram: ䷪ *Guai* 夬 Transform

This hexagram is constructed of one Yin line on top of five Yang lines. It represents a great transformation under way—Yang energy recharging your whole body, like a revolutionary power about to change the entire world.

Body: Stomach organ system, stomach meridian system

The stomach organ system is a Yang Earth Element and the stomach meridian system is *YangMing* with the Yang Bright Dry Metal energy. According to the Five Elements principle, Earth gives birth to and supports Metal. On the other hand, in some situations Metal can help Earth's function by loosening condensed and heavy Yang Earth. When working to strengthen digestive function, it is a good to work with the Metal organs, lung and large intestine, as well as the stomach and large intestine meridian systems.

Numerology: 5 and 10

The Yang Earth number is 5 and the Yin Earth number is 10. Both are used to support the function of Earth.

Alchemical Transformation: *TaiYang HanShui* 太陽寒水
Major Yang Cold Water

According to Chinese cosmology, Chen will transform to *TaiYang*, Major Yang Cold Water, which means the climate pattern will be cold. With respect to Chinese medicine and Daoist internal alchemy, this *TaiYang* Cold Water energy is found in the bladder meridian and small intestine meridian.

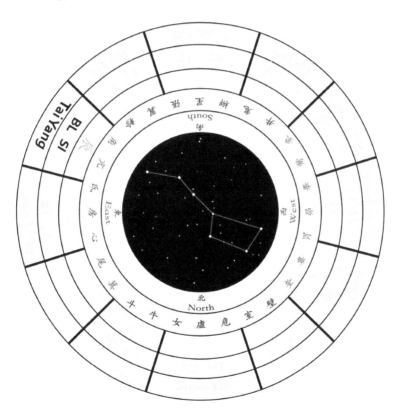

Chen transforms to *TaiYang*, as expressed in the bladder and small intestine meridians.

Figure 71: Chen Alchemical Transformation Diagram

Quality: Power, mystical, healthy, elegant, emotional, thinker

In Chinese astrology, a well-supported Chen person will be powerful, mystical, healthy, and elegant. Out of balance, they may tend towards being over emotional and over thinking. With Chen in the Destiny Palace, the person will be wise and good at making plans.

RenYuan 人元 **(Hidden Stem):** Wu 戊, Gui 癸, Yi 乙

The primary hidden stem is Yang Earth Wu 戊. Chen is the reservoir of Water and it will display the strength of Yin Water Gui if there are other Water Stems and/or its "gangs" (*DiZhiSanHe* 地支三合 Tri-combination Principle—see Section 4.9) in the chart. Chen also represents the last month of the Wood season and it will show its Yin Wood Yi qualities if there is also a good amount of Wood energy in the chart.

LüLü 律呂 **(Musical Pitch):** *GuXian* 姑洗

This vibration of Yang energy supports the growth of strong and pure life energy. The energy of *GuXian* resonates in the stomach meridian Qi. It is equal to the modern musical scale major third or E.

Chen Internal Alchemy Practice: In the GanZhi standing posture, face southeast and visualize yellow color Qi surrounding you and entering into your stomach with the inhalation. With each exhalation, intensify your visualization: imagine your toes are grabbing the earth with more force, close your Earthly Door tighter, reach your fingertips deeper into the earth, and stretch your head taller to reach high into the heavens, all the while paying attention to your stomach meridian. Repeat for a minimum of 49 breaths.

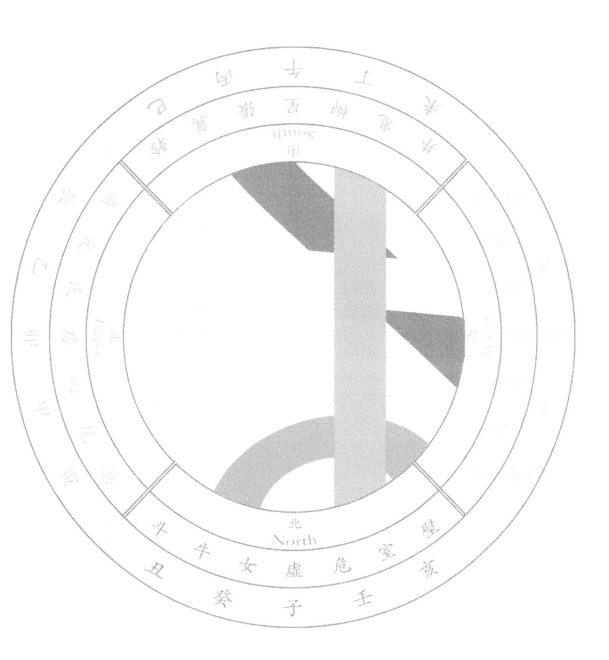

3.6 Si 巳

Si is the sixth Branch. It carries the energy of a plant preparing for its full growth. It also can mean stop—as when a person or plant reaches the state of full maturity and stops physical growth. In its Oracle Script, Si forms the image from the *Yi* 翼 Lunar Mansion in the southern Red Bird celestial region. *Xun* 巽 ☴ Wind is its associated trigram.

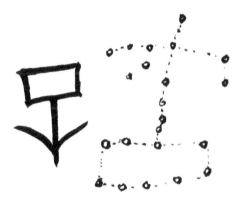

Figure 72: Star pattern—the source of the 巳 character

Element: Fire

Si has a Yin body, which means Si is Yin Fire when it follows the numerological order (6 is a Yin number) and its function is Yang, which means it has an uprising Yang Fire function in other situations.

Spiritual Animal: Snake

The animal sign comes from the spiritual animal of *Yi* Lunar Mansion. Snake represents purity and fully awakened consciousness.

Season: May 6–June 5: *LiXia* 立夏 Establish Summer and *XiaoMan* 小滿 Minor Full

Figure 73: Early Western Zhou Dynasty bronze snake

This is the first month of summer, which also represents a very strong stage of life or the young adult period.

Hour: 09.00–10.59

This is the time for achievement, accomplishments and getting things done.

Direction: Southeast

This is both the spiritual and physical southeast direction, as well as the front-left side of a house or body.

Hexagram: ䷀ *Qian* 乾 Strength

This hexagram has six pure unbroken Yang lines, which symbolize perfection, complete, power, circular, round, and the Heavenly Way.

Body: Small intestine organ system, spleen meridian system

The small intestine organ system is of the Yang Fire Element. The spleen meridian system is *TaiYin*, the Major Yin Damp Earth, which is of the Yin Earth Element. As we can see in nature, wetlands need a good amount of sunny days in order for things to grow in a healthy way. It is the same in the body—the Damp Earth spleen meridian system will function best if it is well supported by the Yang Fire small intestine organ system. Strong sunshine will wither plant life if there is not a reliable source of water, as good damp soil serves as a form of protection against intense heat from the sun. Dampness of the spleen meridian Yin Earth helps balance the Yang Fire of small intestine.

Numerology: 2 and 7

The Yin Fire number is 2 and the Yang Fire number is 7. Both are used to support the function of the Fire Element.

Alchemical Transformation: *JueYin FengMu* 厥陰風木
Reverse Yin Wind Wood

According to Chinese cosmology, Si transforms into the *JueYin*, the Reverse Yin Wind Wood, which suggests a period of strong windstorms. In our bodies, this Wind Wood energy manifests in the pericardium meridian system and liver meridian system.

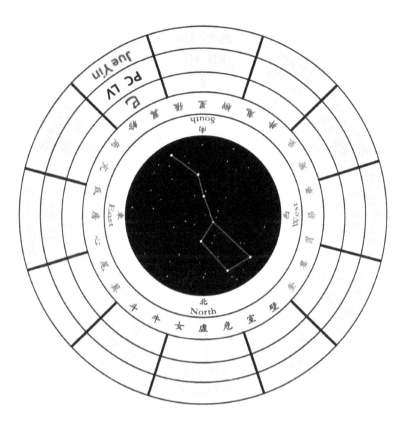

Si transforms to *JueYin*, as expressed in the pericardium and liver meridians.

Figure 74: Si Alchemical Transformation Diagram

Quality: Cautious, intuitive, knowledgeable, attractive, conceited, insatiable, sluggish

In Chinese astrology, a well-supported Si person may be cautious, intuitive, knowledgeable, and attractive, whereas an imbalanced Si person will tend more towards being conceited, insatiable, and sluggish. If Si is in the Destiny Palace, the person may be well educated and lead a life focused on scholarly pursuits.

RenYuan 人元 **(Hidden Stem):** Bing 丙, Wu 戊, Geng 庚

Yang Fire Bing is Si's main hidden Stem. Yang Earth Wu will gain more influence if Si is in a situation in which the Earth Element is strong. Geng Metal will exert its power if Si is surrounded by strong Metal Element energy.

LüLü 律呂 (Musical Pitch): *ZhongLü* 仲呂

The *ZhongLü* energy is that of Yang reaching its peak level, with Yin preparing to begin its ascent. This quality Qi resonates in the spleen meridian of the body. The vibration is similar to that of the perfect fourth of F in the modern musical system.

Si Internal Alchemy Practice: In the GanZhi standing posture, face northeast and visualize red color Qi surrounding you and entering into your small intestine with each inhalation. With each exhalation, intensify your visualization: imagine your toes are grabbing the earth with more force, close your Earthly Door tighter, reach your fingertips deeper into the earth, and stretch your head taller to reach high into the heavens, all the while paying attention to your spleen meridian. Repeat for a minimum of 49 breaths.

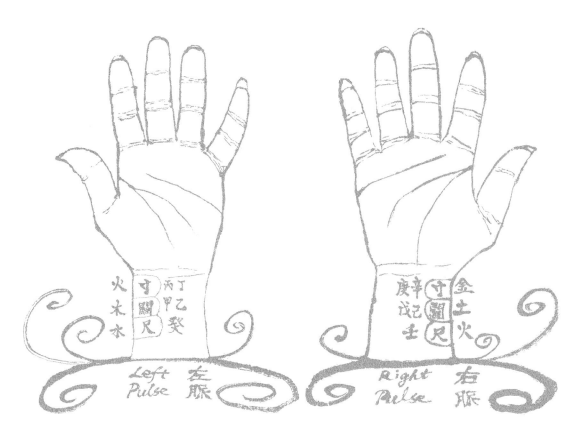

火木水　寸關尺　丁乙癸　丙甲　　左脈　Left Pulse

金土火　寸關尺　辛己　庚戊壬　右脈　Right Pulse

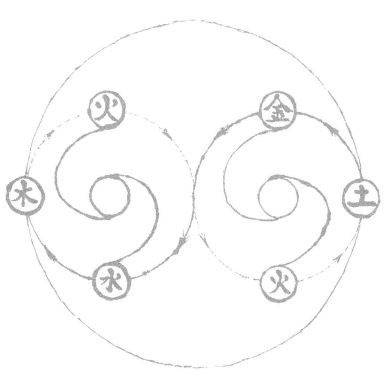

天干五行脈圖

火　金
木　土
水　火

癸巳季夏於瑞典乾元子

3.7 Wu 午

Wu 午 is the seventh Earthly Branch. It means noon, intertwine, or reverse. The Oracle Script is associated with the Lunar Mansions *Zhang* 張 and *Xing* 星 from the southern Red Bird celestial region. *Li* 離 ☲ Fire is its trigram.

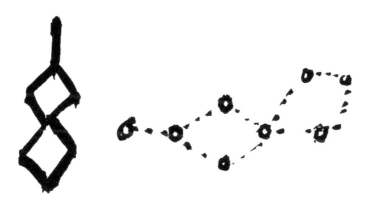

Figure 75: Star pattern—the source of the 午 character

Element: Fire

Wu 午 is characterized as Yang body (physical function) with Yin function (energetic function). Wu 午 shows off its Yang Fire Element nature if it is following the numerological order (7 is a Yang number) and its Yin Fire Element if it is expressing its energetic nature.

Spiritual Animal: Horse

The spiritual animal comes from the Lunar Mansion *Xing* of the Southern Bird celestial region.

Season: June 6–July 7: *MangZhong* 芒種 Plumpy Seed and *XiaZhi* 夏至 Summer Solstice

Figure 76: Bronze horse discovered in a 1800-year-old tomb in XianYang 咸陽 city, ShaanXi province in 2008. It is the largest life-size bronze horse ever found in China, measuring 1.6m (5.3ft) tall and 1.6m (5.3 ft) long.

This is the midsummer time period when nature has fully matured. It signifies the middle age of your life or the peak stage of your career.

Hour: 11.00–12.59

This is the time to nourish your body and heart—it is the best time to eat your lunch and to follow your meal with a gentle Qigong or meditation practice.

Direction: South

Wu 午 represents both the spiritual southern direction, the physical cardinal southern direction, or the front of your house or your body.

Hexagram: ䷫ *Gou* 姤 Copulate

The Gou hexagram has five Yang lines on top of one Yin Line, which symbolizes Yin energy beginning to rise and interact with Yang energy.

Body: Heart organ system, heart meridian system

The heart organ system is of the Fire Element and heart meridian system is *ShaoYin*, the Minor Yin Imperial Fire, which is also of the Fire Element. This is a strong Fire position and it is a good idea to have strong Water to keep the balance. It is a good rule of thumb to work with the kidneys when trying to strengthen your heart function.

Numerology: 2 and 7

The Yin Fire number is 2 and the Yang Fire number is 7. Both are used to strengthen the Fire Element.

Alchemical Transformation: *ShaoYin JunHuo* 少陰君火
Minor Yin Imperial Fire

In alchemical transformation, Wu 午 and Zi are partnered and share the same energetic results. Therefore, the information here is the same as Zi: In Chinese cosmology, Wu 午 Fire transforms to *ShaoYin* (Minor Yin Imperial Fire) energy, which means the climate pattern will heat up and will affect function of the kidney and heart. In the body, the Qi in both the kidney meridian and heart meridian expresses this *ShaoYin* Fire energy. This phenomenon was discussed in the alchemical transformation commentary of the Zi Earthly Branch.

Wu 午 transforms to *ShaoYin*, as expressed in the kidney and heart meridians.

Figure 77: Wu 午 Alchemical Transformation Diagram

Quality: Enduring, powerful, lively, passionate, agitated, irritable, arrogant

In Chinese astrology, a well-supported Wu 午 person will be enduring, powerful, lively, and passionate. When out of balance, the person will tend more towards agitation, irritability, and arrogance. If Wu 午 is in the Destiny Palace, the person is likely to have a rich and easy life.

RenYuan 人元 **(Hidden Stem)**: Ding丁, Ji 己

Ding is the strongest of Wu's 午 hidden Stems. Ji will take charge once there is a strong representation of Earth Element in the chart.

LüLü 律呂 (Musical Pitch): *RuiBin* 蕤賓

The energy of *RuiBin* is that of Yang Qi guiding Yin Qi, combining the YinYang energies together to support the growth of everything. It is the Qi of the heart meridian system of the body. The vibration is equal to the modern musical system triton or G♭/F#.

Wu 午 **Internal Alchemy Practice:** In the GanZhi standing posture, face south and visualize red color Qi surrounding you and entering into your heart with each inhalation. With each exhalation, intensify your visualization: imagine your toes are grabbing the earth with more force, close your Earthly Door tighter, reach your fingertips deeper into the earth, and stretch your head taller to reach high into the heavens, all the while paying attention to your heart meridian. Repeat for a minimum of 49 breaths.

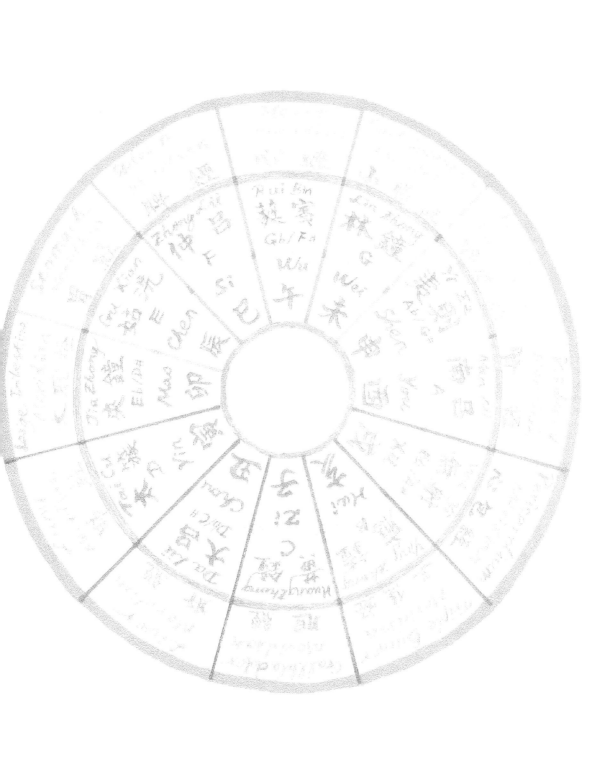

3.8 Wei 未

Wei is the eighth Branch. It means future, deny, or flavor. The Oracle Script is related to the shape of the Lunar Mansion *Jing* 井 in the southern Red Bird celestial region. Its trigram is *Kun* 坤 ☷ Earth.

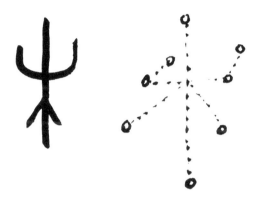

Figure 78: Star pattern—the source of the 未 character

Element: Earth

Wei is Yin Earth Element from all perspectives.

Spiritual Animal: Goat

The spiritual animal is from the Lunar Manson *Gui* in the southern Red Bird region of the celestial realm.

Season: July 7–August 7: *XiaoShu* 小暑 Minor Heat and *DaShu* 大暑 Major Heat

Figure 79: Song Dynasty clay goat

This is the third month of the summer season and it is the hottest time of the year. The plants begin to draw their life energy back into their roots. It is time to prepare for retirement or the late middle-aged stage of life.

Hour: 13.00–14.59

This is the best time of day to take a short nap.

Direction: Southwest

It can be the physical direction of southwest or the front-right of your house or your body.

Hexagram: ䷠ *Dun* 遯 Retreat

The trigram has two Yin lines beneath four Yang lines, which indicates the Yin energy is getting stronger from the previous stage while Yang energy is retreating.

Body: Spleen and pancreas organ systems, small intestine meridian system

In Daoist tradition and classical Chinese medicine, the spleen organ system includes the pancreas. The spleen organ system is of the Earth Element. The small intestine meridian system is *TaiYang*, the Major Yang Cold Water, which is of the Water Element, although the small intestine organ is considered Yang Fire. According to the Daoist internal alchemy principle *SanJiaXiangJian* 三家相見, harmonizing these Three Families (Fire, Water, and Earth) is the essential key to health, longevity, and achieving enlightenment.

Numerology: 5 and 10

The Yang Earth number is 5 and the Yin Earth number is 10. Both are used to help balance the Earth Element.

Alchemical Transformation: *TaiYin ShiTu* 太陰濕土
Major Yin Damp Earth

This is the same as for the Branch Chou. According to Chinese cosmology, Wei transforms *TaiYin*, the Major Yin Damp Earth, which manifests as rain and dampness. This transformation energy is found within the lung meridian system and spleen meridian system of the body. This phenomenon was discussed in the alchemical transformation commentary of the Chou Earthly Branch.

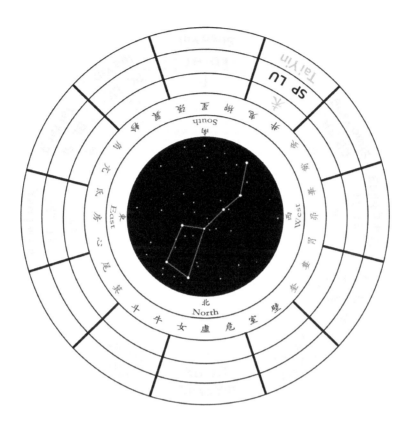

Wei transforms to *TaiYin*, as expressed in the spleen and lung meridians.

Figure 80: Wei Alchemical Transformation Diagram

Quality: Enduring, tender, gracious, charming, sorrowful, imaginary, stubborn

A Wei person shows his or her positive qualities—enduring, tender, gracious, or charming—when in a condition that supports and balances Earth. When Earth is excess or deficient, the person will tend more towards sorrowful, escapist, or stubborn behaviors. A person is destined to be strong and independent if Wei resides in the Destiny Palace.

***RenYuan* 人元 (Hidden Stem):** Yi 乙, Ding 丁, Ji 己

Ji Earth is the most influential hidden Stem. Yi Wood will become strong in situations where the Wood Element becomes strong. Ding Fire will show off its nature when Si is in a powerful Fire environment.

LüLü 律呂 (**Musical Pitch**): *LinZhong* 林鐘

With *LinZhong*, Yin Qi is gaining strength and is better suited to nourishing all things. In the body, it is the Qi of the small intestine system. The vibration is that of the perfect fifth or G in the modern musical system.

Wei Internal Alchemy Practice: From the GanZhi standing posture, face southwest and visualize yellow color Qi surrounding you and entering into your spleen with each inhalation. With each exhalation, intensify your visualization: imagine your toes are grabbing the earth with more force, close your Earthly Door tighter, reach your fingertips deeper into the earth, and stretch your head taller to reach high into the heavens, all the while paying attention to your small intestine meridian. Repeat for a minimum of 49 breaths.

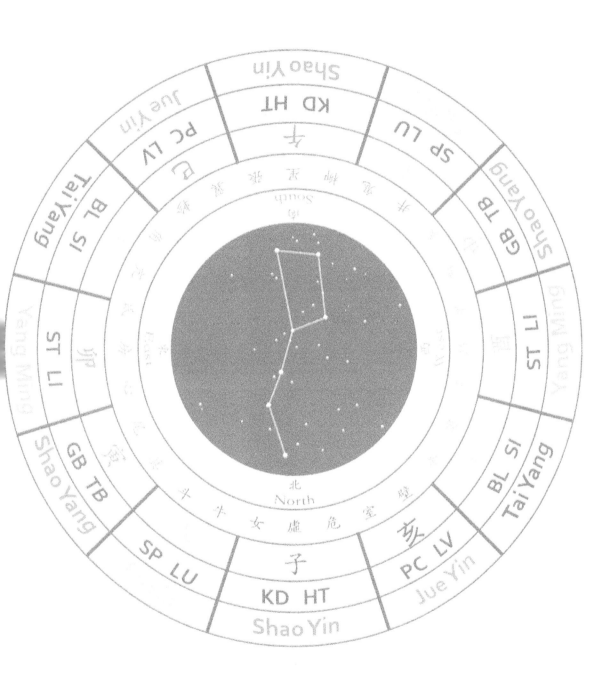

3.9 Shen 申

Shen is the ninth Branch. It means lightening, stretch, express, apply, trust, restrain, report, and spirit. The Oracle Script for Shen is related with the Lunar Mansion *Shen* 參 which resides in the western White Tiger celestial region. The trigram for Shen is *Kun* 坤 ☷ Earth.

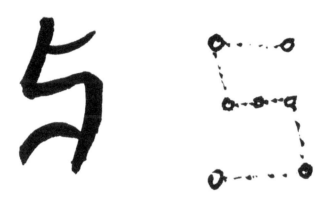

Figure 81: Star pattern—the source of the 申 *character*

Element: Metal

Both physical body and energetic function of Shen is Yang Metal.

Spiritual Animal: Monkey

The spiritual animal is from the Lunar Mansion *Zi* 觜 in the western White Tiger celestial region.

Season: August 8–September 7: *LiQiu* 立秋 Establish Autumn and *ChuShu* 處暑 End Heat

This is the first month of autumn and the time period where the heat of the summer (or of the day, or the life cycle) finally begins to settle down. The natural world continues drawing its Yang energy within as the fruit ripens. This energy symbolizes the fruit of hard labor and the wisdom of experience.

Figure 82: Song Dynasty monkey painting on silk, attributed to the artist MaoSong 毛松

Hour: 15.00–16.59

This is the time to stretch your limits and to persevere so that you may accomplish new things.

Direction: Southwest

This indicates the spiritual and physical southwestern directions or the right-front side of a house or your body.

Hexagram: ☲ *Pi* 否 Break

The *Pi* trigram is made of three Yin lines below three Yang lines. Yin energy continues to increase in strength such that it is now evenly matched with Yang energy. The trigram is a symbol of breaking through old patterns or stagnation in order to achieve a new way of living your life or to reach enlightenment.

Body: Large intestine organ system, bladder meridian system

The large intestine organ system is of the Yang Metal Element. The bladder meridian system is *TaiYang*, Major Yang Cold Water, which is of the Water Element. In order to strengthen the function of both your kidney and bladder systems, it is beneficial to work on improving the function of your large intestine function (and vice versa).

Numerology: 4 and 9

The Yin Metal number is 4 and the Yang Metal number is 9. Both are used to strengthen the function of the Metal Element.

Alchemical Transformation: *ShaoYang XiangHuo* 少陽相火
Minor Yang Ministerial Fire

As with Yin 寅 Tiger, Shen manifests as *ShaoYang* energy (Minor Yang Ministerial Fire) in the Chinese cosmological system, which is a basis for predicting that the climate pattern will bring heat. In our body, *ShaoYang* Ministerial Fire represents the energies of the gallbladder meridian system and triple burner meridian system. This phenomenon was discussed in the alchemical transformation commentary of the Yin 寅 Earthly Branch.

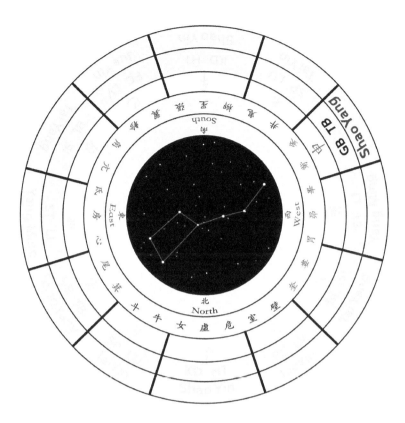

Shen transforms to *ShaoYang*, as expressed in the gallbladder and triple burner meridians.

Figure 83: Shen Alchemical Transformation Diagram

Quality: Spiritual, stretch, expand, intelligent, attentive, spontaneous, elegant, wise, opportunistic, rushed

According to the principles of Chinese astrology, a balanced Shen person carries strong spiritual, intelligent, and elegant energy. Excess or deficiency will bring him or her out of balance and with it characteristics such as opportunism and hastiness follow. If Shen is in the Destiny Palace, the person might feel a great deal of emotional and/or physical distance from his/her family.

RenYuan 人元 **(Hidden Stem):** Wu 戊, Geng 庚, Ren 壬

Geng is the strongest influence of these hidden Stems. Wu 戊 will display its function as long as a strong Earth environment prevails. Ren will rise to power when Shen is immersed in the Water Element.

LüLü 律呂 (Musical Pitch): *YiZe* 夷則

This frequency represents the time when Yang energy has declined to reach a YinYang balance point. The growing Yin energy cuts off the Yang, making everything even. In the body, the Qi of *YiZe* resonates within the bladder meridian system. In the modern musical system, it is equal to the minor six or A♭/G# tone.

Shen Internal Alchemy Practice: In the GanZhi standing posture, face southwest and visualize white color Qi surrounding you and entering into your large intestine with each inhalation. With each exhalation, intensify your visualization: imagine your toes are grabbing the earth with more force, close your Earthly Door tighter, reach your fingertips deeper into the earth, and stretch your head taller to reach high into the heavens, all the while paying attention to your bladder meridian. Repeat for a minimum of 49 breaths.

運化全乎心

宇宙立於手

The Universe is within my hand
and is manifested through my heart.

坤 剝 觀 否 遯 姤 乾 夬 壯 泰 臨 復
Kun Bo Guan Pi Dun Gou Qian Guai Dazhuang Tai Lin Fu

The Wave of Life

3.10 You 酉

You is the tenth Branch. It means wine, fermentation, pond, and mature. The Oracle Script is related to the Lunar Mansions *Mao* 昴 and *Bi* 壁 in the White Tiger celestial region. The trigram for You is *Dui* 兌 ☱ Lake (Marsh).

Figure 84: Star pattern—the source of the 酉 character

Element: Metal

You is Yin Metal Element from all perspectives, both physically and energetically.

Spiritual Animal: Rooster

The spiritual animal comes from *Mao* 昴 Lunar Mansion in the White Tiger celestial region.

Season: September 8–October 7: *BaiLu* 白露 White Dew and *QiuFen* 穐分 Autumn Equinox

You represents the middle month of the autumn. Fruits are ripening as autumn leaves change to bright hues of gold, orange, and red. This is the time for harvest and it also symbolizes the golden years or retirement stage of life.

Figure 85: Han Dynasty clay rooster

Hour: 17.00–18.59

This is the best time of day to enjoy a light evening meal followed by a short internal alchemy meditation practice.

Direction: West

This represents both the spiritual and physical western direction as well as the right side of a building or your body.

Hexagram: ䷓ *Guan* 觀 Observe

The Guan hexagram has two Yang lines on top of four Yin lines, indicating that Yang energy is moving further into its retreat as Yin energy takes hold.

Body: Lung organ system, kidney meridian system

The lung organ system is of the Metal Element. Although the kidney organ is of the Water Element, the kidney meridian system is *ShaoYin* (Minor Yin Imperial Fire), which belongs to the Fire Element. Lung Metal gives birth to the kidney Water. The true Fire hidden within the kidney can refine lung Metal.

Numerology: 4 and 9

The Yin Metal number is 4 and the Yang Metal number is 9. Both are used to strengthen the function of the Metal Element.

Alchemical Transformation: *YangMing ZaoJin* 陽明燥金
Yang Brightness Dry Metal

As discussed previously in the Mao alchemical transformation commentary, in Chinese cosmology, You transforms to *YangMing* (Yang Brightness Dry Metal), which indicates the climatic pattern that is very dry with a lack of rain and moisture. In our body, the Dry Metal energy manifests in the large intestine meridian and stomach meridian. This phenomenon was discussed in the alchemical transformation commentary of the Mao Earthly Branch.

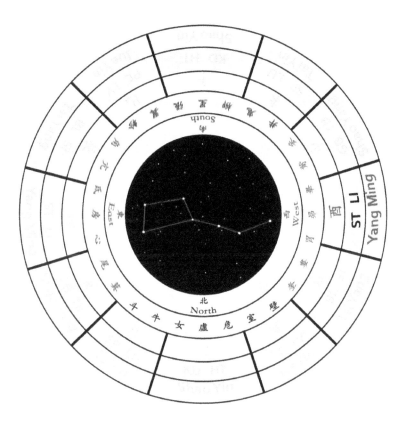

You transforms to *YangMing*, as expressed in the stomach and large intestine meridians.

Figure 86: You Alchemical Transformation Diagram

Quality: Stylish, influential, faithful, humor, alert, arrogant, proud

In Chinese astrology, a healthy You Metal person is stylish, influential, faithful, honorable, and alert, with a tendency towards excess pride and arrogance when out of balance. If You is in the Destiny Palace, the person may be very strong minded and can be self-centered or bossy.

RenYuan 人元 **(Hidden Stem):** Xin 辛

You represents the western cardinal position and holds only Xin Metal within.

LüLü 律呂 **(Musical Pitch):** *NanLü* 南呂

The *NanLü* musical pitch represents Yin Qi as it continues its advance. The vibration of *NanLü* helps nature complete its ripening and fermentation process. In the body, it is the Qi of the kidney meridian system. In the modern musical system it is equivalent to the major sixth or A tone.

You Internal Alchemy Practice: In the GanZhi standing posture, face west and visualize white color Qi surrounding you and entering into your lungs with each inhalation. With each exhalation, intensify your visualization: imagine your toes are grabbing the earth with more force, close your Earthly Door tighter, reach your fingertips deeper into the earth, and stretch your head taller to reach high into the heavens, all the while paying attention to your kidney meridian. Repeat for a minimum of 49 breaths.

3.11 Xü 戌

Xü is the eleventh Branch. It means destroy or dismiss. The Oracle Script is derived from the image of the *Kui* 奎 Lunar Mansion in the western White Tiger celestial region. The associated trigram is *Qian* 乾 ☰ Heaven.

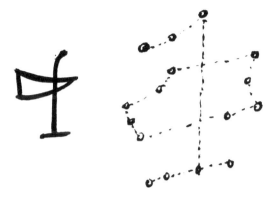

Figure 87: Star pattern—the source of the 戌 character

Element: Earth

Both the physical body and energetic function of Xü is Yang Earth.

Spiritual Animal: Dog

Xü is the spiritual animal of the *Lou* Lunar Mansion in the White Tiger celestial region. Dog symbolizes honesty, trust, and guardianship.

Season: October 8–November 6: *HanLu* 寒露 Cold Dew and *ShuangJiang* 霜降 Frost Descend

This is the last month of the autumn season. Yang energy completes its return to its root as the golden leaves fall to the ground. It represents the elderly phase of life, when one is completely retired.

Figure 88: Han Dynasty clay dog with green glaze

Hour: 19.00–20.59

This is the best time for reading, making or listening to music, playing games, and relaxing.

Direction: Northwest

Xü represents both the spiritual and physical northwestern direction. or the right-back side of a building or your body.

Hexagram: ䷖ *Bo* 剝 Peel

The Bo hexagram has one Yang line on top of five Yin lines. This is the image of Yin energy becoming so strong that it pares away the Yang energy, leaving the illusion that no life energy remains.

Body: Stomach organ system, pericardium meridian system

The stomach organ is of the Yang Earth Element. The pericardium meridian is *JueYin* (Reverse Yin Wind Wood), which is of the Wood Element. Stomach organ Earth and pericardium meridian Wood hold and support each other.

Numerology: 5 and 10

The Yang Earth number is 5 and the Yin Earth number is 10. Both are used to support the function of the Earth Element.

Alchemical Transformation: *TaiYang HanShui* 太陽寒水
Major Yang Cold Water

According to Chinese cosmology, Xü will transform to *TaiYang*, Major Yang Cold Water, which means the climate pattern will be cold. With respect to Chinese medicine and Daoist internal alchemy, this *TaiYang* Cold Water energy is found in the bladder meridian and small intestine meridian. This phenomenon was discussed in the alchemical transformation commentary of the Chen Earthly Branch.

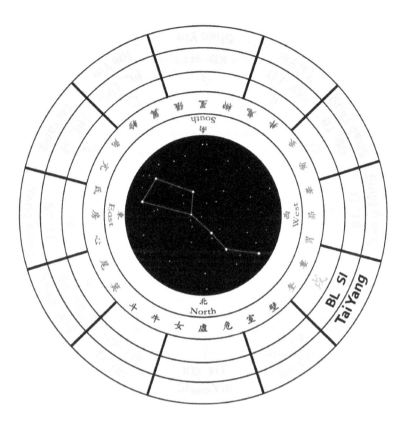

Xü transforms to *TaiYang*, as expressed in the bladder and small intestine meridians.

Figure 89: Xü Alchemical Transformation Diagram

Quality: Intuitive, artistic, cautious, social, honest, loyal, nerves, evasive, stubborn

In the Chinese astrological chart, a balanced Xü person may have great intuitive skills, and be artistic, honest, and loyal. When out of balance, he or she may have a tendency to become stubborn, nervous, and evasive. If Xü is in the Destiny Palace, the person will exhibit truly inspiring creative and artistic energy.

RenYuan 人元 **(Hidden Stem)**: Ding 丁, Wu 戊, Xin 辛

Wu 戊 is the strongest of Xü's hidden Stems. Ding will gather momentum if Xü is supported by strong Fire Elements while Xin will display its influence if Xü is supported by strong Metal Elements.

LüLü 律呂 **(Musical Pitch)**: *WuYi* 無射

The energy of *WuYi* expresses Yang Qi as it completes its cycle and prepares to begin anew. The quality of *WuYi* energy can be found in the pericardium meridian system. The Western equivalent vibration is the minor seventh or B♭/A# tone.

Xü Internal Alchemy Practice: In the GanZhi standing posture, face northwest and visualize yellow color Qi surrounding you and entering into your stomach with each inhalation. With each exhalation, intensify your visualization: imagine your toes are grabbing the earth with more force, close your Earthly Door tighter, reach your fingertips deeper into the earth, and stretch your head taller to reach high into the heavens, all the while paying attention to your pericardium meridian. Repeat for a minimum of 49 breaths.

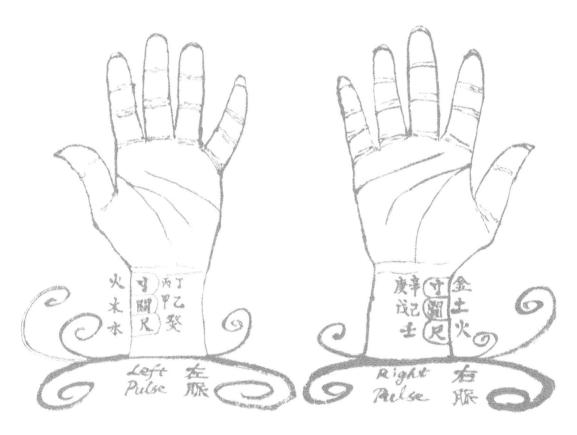

左脈 Left Pulse

火 寸 丙 丁
水 關 甲 乙
水 尺 癸

右脈 Right Pulse

金 寸 土
土 關 己 火
金 尺 戊 辛
庚 壬

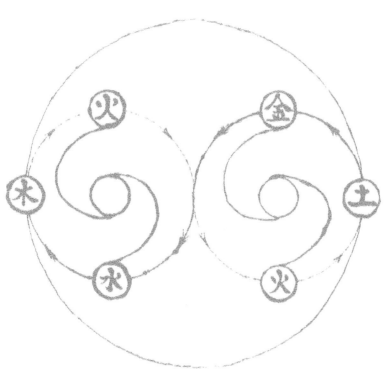

天干五行脈圖

癸巳季夏於瑞興
范大子

3.12 Hai 亥

Hai is the twelfth Branch. It means the roots of grass and pig. The Oracle Script is related to the Lunar Mansions *Bi* 壁, *Shi* 室 and their neighboring asterism *Li* 離. The trigram for Hai is *Qian* 乾 ≡ Heaven.

Figure 90: Star pattern—the source of the 亥 character

Element: Water

Hai has a Yin body with Yang function. By numerological order, Hai is physically Yin Water. With respect to Chinese astrology, it energetically interacts with the other Elements as Yang Water.

Spiritual Animal: Pig

Hai is the spiritual animal of the *Shi* Lunar Mansion in the celestial region of the northern Mystical Warrior.

Season: November 7–December 6: *LiDong* 立冬 Establish Winter and *XiaoXue* 小雪 Minor Snow

This is the first month of the winter season. During this time of year, some animals will already be preparing for

Figure 91: Over-7000-year-old boar engraved on a clay container from HeMuDu 河姆渡 historical site, near YuYao 余姚 in ZheJiang 浙江 province

hibernation and plants draw their life energy back deep into their root system. This represents the end stage of a life cycle and is the time to prepare for a peaceful transition.

Hour: 21.00–22.59

This is the best time to stop all physical and mental activities and go to sleep!

Direction: Northwest

This can represent both the spiritual and physical northwestern direction or it can be the back-right side of a building or your body.

Hexagram: ䷁ *Kun* 坤 Flow

The *Kun* hexagram contains six pure Yin lines—Yin energy has now taken over and is completely dominant.

Body: Bladder organ system, triple burner meridian system

The bladder organ is Yang Water and the triple burner meridian is *ShaoYang* (Minor Yang Ministerial Fire), which is the Fire Element. Working with these two systems together in a correct way helps bring the whole body YinYang energy into balance.

Numerology: 1 and 6

As with Zi, the number 1 represents Yang Water and the number 6 represents Yin Water. Both are used to support the Water Element.

Alchemical Transformation: *JueYin FengMu* 厥陰風木
Reverse Yin Wind Wood

According to Chinese cosmology, Hai transforms into the *JueYin*, the Reverse Yin Wind Wood, which suggests a period with strong windstorms. In our bodies, this Wind Wood energy manifests in the pericardium meridian system and liver meridian system. This phenomenon was discussed in the alchemical transformation commentary of the Si Earthly Branch.

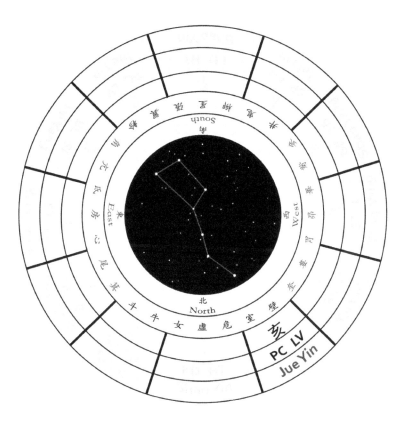

Hai transforms to *JueYin*, as expressed in the pericardium and liver meridians.

Figure 92: Hai Alchemical Transformation Diagram

Quality: Gentle, knowledgeable, joyful, smart, honest, trustworthy, brave, angry, insecure, unstable

In Chinese astrology, a balanced Hai person may be gentle, joyful, smart, and honest, whereas imbalance will lead to insecurity and instability. If Hai is in the Destiny Palace, expect to see someone with great sympathy and compassion and a willingness to help others.

RenYuan 人元 **(Hidden Stem):** Jia 甲, Ren 壬

Ren is the predominant Hidden Stem. Jia gains strength when Hai is in a powerful Wood energy situation.

LüLü 律呂 (Musical Pitch): *YingZhong* 應鐘

Yin Qi reaches its peak level and starts to generate Yang Qi. This is the resonance of conception. The Qi of the triple burner meridian system within the body vibrates with *YingZhong* energy. In the Western system, it correlates to the major seventh or B tone.

Hai Internal Alchemy Practice: In the GanZhi standing posture, face northwest and visualize mystical Qi (like moon light or the northern lights) surrounding you and entering into your bladder with each inhalation. With each exhalation, intensify your visualization: imagine your toes are grabbing the earth with more force, close your Earthly Door tighter, reach your fingertips deeper into the earth, and stretch your head taller to reach high into the heavens, all the while paying attention to your triple burner meridian. Repeat for a minimum of 49 breaths.

Figure 93: Shui 水 *people's twelve animals coin*
The twelve animals of the Chinese zodiac are shown near the outer rim. The names of the twelve Earthly Branches are found written in *ShuiShu* (*Shui* Script) around the center hole. *Shui* itself means "water." The *Shui* people of China live near rivers and streams and much of their customs and folklore revolves around water. *ShuiShu* uses pictographs that are similar to the ancient characters *JiaGuWen* 甲骨文 found on the oracle bones from the Shang Dynasty (personal collection of LiuChunSheng 劉春聲).

Figure 94: Twelve Earthly Branches Alchemical Transformation Diagram
In Daoism, the Big Dipper represents the center of the universe. Its rotation in relation to the 28 Lunar Mansions marks the changing seasons and the transformation of universal energies.

千禧文化

癸巳仲夏吉日
乾元之子 於瑞典

4

GanZhi HeHua 干支合化

Stems, Branches and Alchemical Transformation

We provided you with a great deal of the symbolic associations of the GanZhi in Chapters 2 and 3. In this chapter, we will first review the basic Five Elements birth and control principles and then move on to focus on the more complex GanZhi Five Elements alchemical transformation principles. After you give yourself some time to study these essential principles of alchemical processes, you may gain further insight into the information in the previous chapters.

4.1 *WuXingXiangSheng* 五行相生 **Birth Principle**

The generating or birth principle is one of the two main relationships that steer the movement of the Five Elements. Each Element is intimately bonded to just one other by this principle. In this cycle, Water nourishes Wood, Wood gives rise to (fuels) Fire, Fire begets (creates, through ash) Earth, Earth produces (bears) Metal, and Metal gives birth to (carries) Water.

The birth relationship between two Elements fluctuates, and can bring either helpful or detrimental effects. Generally speaking, in this "parent–child" dynamic, the child element will drain some amount of energy from its parent element. For example, if the child (Wood) is currently in need of support, the parent (Water) will pour forth its energy in a nourishing way. However, it may happen that the child is currently too strong (for example, an overindulged child) and will not benefit from a cosseting parent. It is also possible that the child is too weak (for example, an excessively timid child who needs to learn independence) to profit from a domineering parent. When Water burdens

Wood, we say *ShuiDuoMuPiao* 水多木漂—an overabundance of Water causes Wood to drift away. Similarly, we have phrases to describe the harmful effects of the other birth relationships: *MuDuoHuoXi* 木多火熄—overloading Wood will suffocate Fire, *HuoDuoTuJiao* 火多土焦—raging Fire scorches Earth, *TuDuoJinMai* 土多金埋—excess Earth will bury Metal, and *JinDuoShuiZhuo* 金多水濁—a glut of Metal pollutes Water.

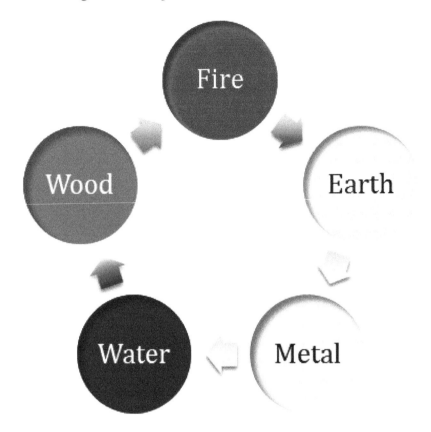

Figure 95: Conventional Five Elements Birth Relationship Diagram

4.2 *WuXingXiangKe* 五行相克 Control Principle

There are other balancing relationships within the Five Elements known as controlling relationships. These may also help or hinder, depending on the specific circumstances. According to the control principle, Water extinguishes Fire, Fire refines Metal, Metal controls Wood, Wood penetrates Earth, and Earth channels Water.

Traditionally, the controlling relationship has been likened to a "grandparent–grandchild" relationship. Although family dynamics are changing rapidly in China, up until about 40 years ago, it was very common for most people to live in multigenerational homes. The role of the grandparent was that of the disciplinarian, especially with respect to the oldest grandson, who was responsible for carrying the family lineage forward. Depending on the age of the child, it could take a significant amount of the grandfather's energy to keep his grandson in check. In this dynamic, the energy is drained from both the controlling and the controlled Element.

It is also possible to have a backlash reaction in which the controlled Element "reverse-controls" the controlling Element. This happens when the force of controlled Element is very strong. For example, when Water controls Fire, Water becomes weaker because it is giving its own energy to restrain the Fire. However, if the Fire is too strong to succumb to the cooling Water, the tides turn, and Fire will dry up the Water. As in any relationship, the interaction between the Elements is ever changing and mutually experienced.

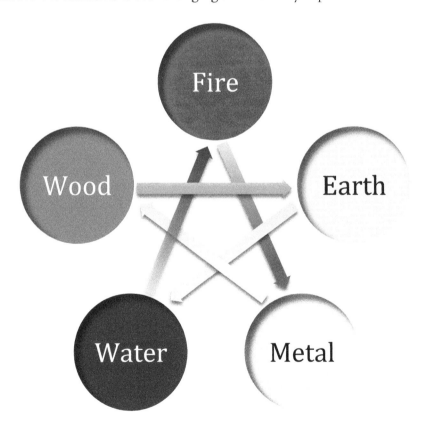

Figure 96: Conventional Five Elements Control Relationship Diagram

4.3 *TianGan WuXing Mai Tu* 天干五行脈圖
Heavenly Stems Five Elements Pulse Diagram

Pulse reading is one of the most important diagnostic tools in traditional Chinese medicine. Chinese medicine doctors gain insight into the internal workings of the body by assessing three pulse positions on each wrist. As Figure 97 shows, these positions are associated with the Heavenly Stems:

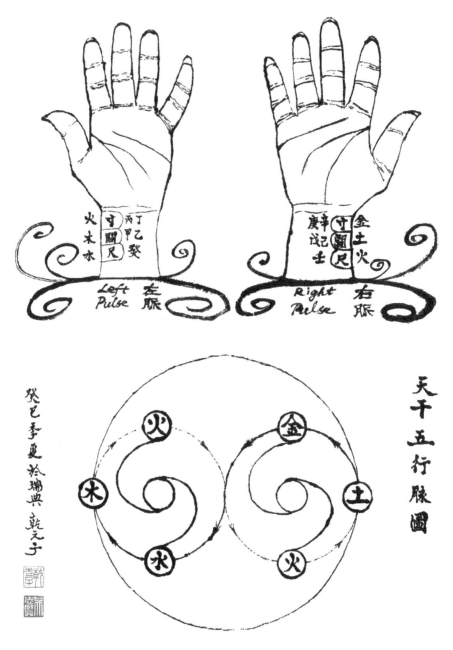

Figure 97: Heavenly Stems Five Elements Pulse Diagram

- *ZuoChi* 左尺—Bottom Left Water (furthest from wrist crease): Gui (left kidney)

- *ZuoGuan* 左關—Middle Left Wood: Jia (gallbladder) and Yi (liver)

- *ZuoCun* 左寸—Top Left Imperial Fire: Bing (small intestine) and Ding (heart)

- *YouChi* 右尺—Bottom Right Ministerial Fire, hidden within Water: Ren (bladder and right kidney)

- *YouGuan* 右關—Middle Right Earth: Wu 戊 (stomach) and Ji (spleen/pancreas)

- *YouCun* 右寸—Top Right Metal: Geng (large intestine) and Xin (lung)

When we apply the Five Elements creation principles to the location of the pulse points, an image of an infinity formed by double Taiji symbols is formed: Water (bottom left position) gives birth to Wood (middle left position); Wood gives birth to Fire (top left position); Imperial Fire resonates with Ministerial Fire, which is hidden within Water (bottom right); Fire gives birth to Earth (middle right), Earth gives birth to Metal (top right), Metal gives birth to Water (bottom left), and so on. This pattern reminds us of the fundamental principle of Chinese medicine: we achieve a state of health and well being when our Qi (vital energy) courses smoothly and continuously throughout our body. Any weakness or blockage of our Qi will reveal itself through specific pulse qualities at its related position. Guided by the symbolism of the Heavenly Stems, highly skilled Chinese medicine doctors are able to diagnose the current state of health, divine the entire health history, and make predictions regarding health, love, family, occupation, financial success and future outcomes through their pulse reading techniques. You can find details of this mystical style of pulse reading in *TaiSuMaiMiJue* 太素脈秘訣 (TaiSu's Secrets of the Pulse), one of the Daoist classics of Chinese pulse diagnosis.

4.4 *WuShiWuXingHuaTu* 吳氏五行化圖
Wu Family Five Elements Transformation Diagram

It is important to understand that Earth is the central Element that cooperates with all Elements, especially when using the Five Elements knowledge to guide your clinical or internal cultivation practice. Thousands of years before the first telescopes and microscopes, ancient sages, with acutely refined senses, were able to use their physical bodies to observe nature, map the sky and perceive their inner realms. Daoist temples, traditionally called *Guan* 觀 (observation), were havens to contemplate the natural phenomena in the outer world and the patterns of subtle energies within the body. From an inner cultivation perspective, you are the center of the universe—your body is the reference point for your internal and external observation. On a macrocosmic scale, the Earth, the observational standpoint for those who live here and observe all that exists, is the center of the universe.

The *HuaiNanZhi* 淮南子, a Chinese philosophical classic from the 2nd century BCE, elegantly defines the universe as *YuZhou* 宇宙. *Yu* 宇 means space (six directions: above, below, and the four cardinal directions) and *Zhou* 宙 means time (past, present, and future). Without a center point of reference, there can be no distinction of direction, which according to the *HuaiNanZhi*, is necessary to define the universe. In Daoism, Earth is the center around which everything in the universe turns. The Earth also represents yourself and your *DanTian* 丹田—the elixir field of life energy in your lower belly. The four seasons correspond to the four directions, and Earth is found within each of them. *TuWangSiJi* 土旺四季 is a key Five Elements principle—Earth prospers in all seasons. The Five Elements represent the way of nature and the wheel of life, with Earth holding the central axis, in constant synergy with the other Elements.

As shown in Figures 95 and 96, the conventional Five Elements birth and control relationship diagrams are convenient tools for learning and memorizing two primary connections of the Elements. However, it is inherently flawed as it fails to establish the pivotal role of the Earth in the Five Elements principle. Through our own cultivation practice, we have seen how to create a diagram (see Figure 98) that recovers the original interaction of the Five Elements birth/control relationships.

As you can see, we have restored the Earth as the central axis. In accordance with the fundamental principles of Daoism, you will see the Fire at the top, in the Yang Qi position; Water, the repository for Yin energy, at the bottom; Wood, the ascending pathway of Yang Qi, on the left; and Metal, the descending pathway of Yin Qi, on the right. In each Element, we have chosen dark and light colors to express the Yin and Yang qualities of each Element. We used solid lines to demonstrate the generation or birth relationship, and broken lines show the direction of the controlling relationship.

Bringing these two principles together, it becomes clear that both Oracle Script characters, *Wu* (Five) and *Xing* (Element), are revealed within the shape of the diagram itself. The Wu Family Five Elements Transformation Diagram helps elucidate the continuous interplay between the three primary principles of the Five Elements, generating life, promoting optimal health, and ideally, creating a harmonious world.

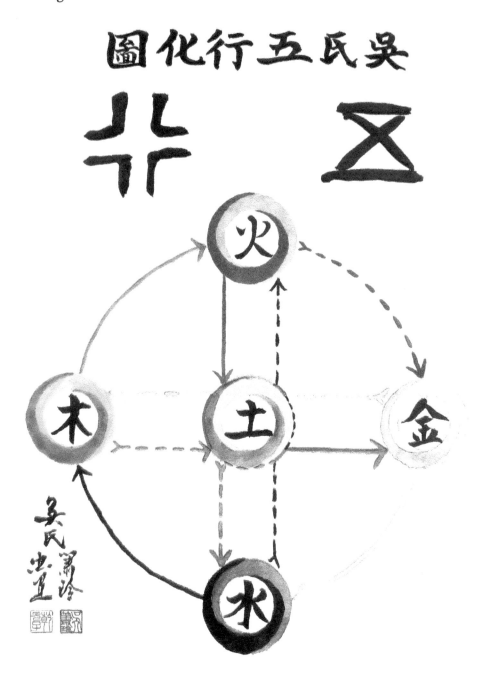

Figure 98: Wu Family Five Elements Transformation Diagram

4.5 *TianGanHeHua* 天干合化
Heavenly Stems Transformation Principle

As discussed in the *HuangDiNeiJing*, there are five special pairs of different Stem combinations that do not follow the Five Elements generation or control principles. Instead, when the following pairs come together they have the potential to alchemically transform and create a new Elemental energy. This transformation happens continuously throughout nature. Here is a small example: when hydrogen and oxygen (note: all gases are considered to have predominantly "metal" qualities) come together with a sudden spark of energy (fire), water is created—*BingXinHeHuaShui* 丙辛合化水.

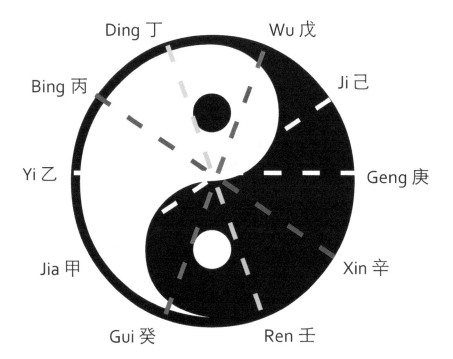

Figure 99: Heavenly Stems Transformation Principle

戊 丁 丙 乙 甲
癸 壬 辛 庚 己
合 合 合 合 合
化 化 化 化 化
火 木 水 金 土

JiaJiHeHuaTu
YiGengHeHuaJin
BingXinHeHuaShui
DingRenHeHuaMu
WuGuiHeHuaHuo

Jia Yang Wood and Ji Yin Earth transform into Earth
Yi Yin Wood and Geng Yang Metal transform into Metal
Bing Yang Fire and Xin Yin Metal transform into Water
Ding Yin Fire and Ren Yang Water transform into Wood
Wu Yang Earth and Gui Yin Water transform into Fire

4.6 *WuYun* 五運 Five Cosmological Energies

WuYun 五運 is a Chinese term that specifically refers to the Five Elements' cosmological transformative energies that occur during the annual energetic cycle. These energies are calculated according to the Heavenly Stems of the Chinese calendar and are named Wood, Fire, Earth, Metal, and Water (please note that the *Yun* concept of cosmological energies is different from the Five Elements concept of Wood, Fire, Earth, Metal, and Water). Insight into the use of the *WuYun* 五運 and *LiuQi* 六氣 (see Section 4.11) for predictions about climate patterns and how different cosmological energies affect the functioning of human beings come from Chapters 66–71 and 74 of the *HuangDiNeiJing*.

The *WuYun* have two parts, the *ZhuYun* 主運 (host *Yun*) and *KeYun* 客運 (guest *Yun*). The five energies of the host *Yun* follow the same order every year: Wood, Fire, Earth, Metal, and Water. The order of guest *Yun* will change every year according to its Stem's transformation pattern (see Section 4.5). Traditionally, we use the pentatonic scale (see Section 1.7 *QiYun* 氣韵 The Rhythm of Qi) to describe the quality of each *Yun*. These musical tones embody the energetic characteristic of each *Yun*. To help learn each Stem's host and guest *Yun*, we list the details in Table 6.

Table 6: Five cosmological energies

WuYun 五運	Heavenly Stem	*ZhuKe* 主客	Musical tone of each phase of the annual energetic cycle				
			1st	2nd	3rd	4th	5th
Tu 土 **Earth**	Jia 甲	Host	*Jue* 角 Wood	*Zhi* 徵 Fire	*Gong* 宮 Earth	*Shang* 商 Metal	*Yü* 羽 Water
			Excess	Deficient	Excess	Deficient	Excess
		Guest	*Gong* 宮 Earth	*Shang* 商 Metal	*Yü* 羽 Water	*Jue* 角 Wood	*Zhi* 徵 Fire
			Excess	Deficient	Excess	Deficient	Excess
	Ji 己	Host	*Jue* 角 Wood	*Zhi* 徵 Fire	*Gong* 宮 Earth	*Shang* 商 Metal	*Yü* 羽 Water
			Deficient	Excess	Deficient	Excess	Deficient
		Guest	*Gong* 宮 Earth	*Shang* 商 Metal	*Yü* 羽 Water	*Jue* 角 Wood	*Zhi* 徵 Fire
			Deficient	Excess	Deficient	Excess	Deficient
Jin 金 **Metal**	Yi 乙	Host	*Jue* 角 Wood	*Zhi* 徵 Fire	*Gong* 宮 Earth	Shang 商 Metal	*Yü* 羽 Water
			Excess	Deficient	Excess	Deficient	Excess
		Guest	Shang 商 Metal	*Yü* 羽 Water	*Jue* 角 Wood	*Zhi* 徵 Fire	*Gong* 宮 Earth
			Deficient	Excess	Deficient	Excess	Deficient
	Geng 庚	Host	*Jue* 角 Wood	*Zhi* 徵 Fire	*Gong* 宮 Earth	*Shang* 商 Metal	*Yü* 羽 Water
			Deficient	Excess	Deficient	Excess	Deficient
		Guest	Shang 商 Metal	*Yü* 羽 Water	*Jue* 角 Wood	*Zhi* 徵 Fire	*Gong* 宮 Earth
			Excess	Deficient	Excess	Deficient	Excess

Shui 水 **Water**	**Bing** 丙	Host	*Jue* 角 Wood	*Zhi* 徵 Fire	*Gong* 宮 Earth	Shang 商 Metal	*Yü* 羽 Water
			Excess	Deficient	Excess	Deficient	Excess
		Guest	*Yü* 羽 Water	*Jue* 角 Wood	*Zhi* 徵 Fire	*Gong* 宮 Earth	Shang 商 Metal
			Excess	Deficient	Excess	Deficient	Excess
	Xin 辛	Host	*Jue* 角 Wood	*Zhi* 徵 Fire	*Gong* 宮 Earth	Shang 商 Metal	*Yü* 羽 Water
			Deficient	Excess	Deficient	Excess	Deficient
		Guest	*Yü* 羽 Water	*Jue* 角 Wood	*Zhi* 徵 Fire	*Gong* 宮 Earth	Shang 商 Metal
			Deficient	Excess	Deficient	Excess	Deficient
Mu 木 **Wood**	Ding 丁	Host	*Jue* 角 Wood	*Zhi* 徵 Fire	*Gong* 宮 Earth	Shang 商 Metal	*Yü* 羽 Water
			Deficient	Excess	Deficient	Excess	Deficient
		Guest	*Jue* 角 Wood	*Zhi* 徵 Fire	*Gong* 宮 Earth	Shang 商 Metal	*Yü* 羽 Water
			Deficient	Excess	Deficient	Excess	Deficient
	Ren 壬	Host	*Jue* 角 Wood	*Zhi* 徵 Fire	*Gong* 宮 Earth	Shang 商 Metal	*Yü* 羽 Water
			Excess	Deficient	Excess	Deficient	Excess
		Guest	*Jue* 角 Wood	*Zhi* 徵 Fire	*Gong* 宮 Earth	Shang 商 Metal	*Yü* 羽 Water
			Excess	Deficient	Excess	Deficient	Excess
Huo 火 **Fire**	Wu 戊	Host	*Jue* 角 Wood	*Zhi* 徵 Fire	*Gong* 宮 Earth	Shang 商 Metal	*Yü* 羽 Water
			Deficient	Excess	Deficient	Excess	Deficient
		Guest	*Zhi* 徵 Fire	*Gong* 宮 Earth	Shang 商 Metal	*Yü* 羽 Water	*Jue* 角 Wood
			Excess	Deficient	Excess	Deficient	Excess
	Gui 癸	Host	*Jue* 角 Wood	*Zhi* 徵 Fire	*Gong* 宮 Earth	Shang 商 Metal	*Yü* 羽 Water
			Excess	Deficient	Excess	Deficient	Excess
		Guest	*Zhi* 徵 Fire	*Gong* 宮 Earth	Shang 商 Metal	*Yü* 羽 Water	*Jue* 角 Wood
			Deficient	Excess	Deficient	Excess	Deficient

4.7 *DiZhiLiuHe* 地支六合
Earthly Branches Six Unions Principle

Similarly, there are six couplings of Earthly Branches that also may transform into a new energetic Elemental pattern.

Figure 100: Earthly Branches Six Unions Principle

午 巳 辰 卯 寅 子
未 申 酉 戌 亥 丑
合 合 合 合 合 合
土 水 金 火 木 土

ZiChouHeTu
YinHaiHeMu
MaoXüHeHuo
ChenYouHeJin
SiShenHeShui
WuWeiHeTu

Zi and Chou transform into Earth
Yin and Hai transform into Wood
Mao and Xü transform into Fire
Chen and You transform into Metal
Si and Shen transform into Water
Wu and Wei transform into Earth

4.8 *DiZhiSanHui* 地支三會
Earthly Branches Tri-gathering Principle

The twelve Earthly Branches can also be divided into groups based on directional energy. Any time the directional triplet of Branches is found together, the effect of the associated Elemental energy grows exponentially. For example, when all the Southern Branches occur simultaneously as they would in the Wei 未 day of the Wu 午 month of the Si 巳 year (e.g. June 10, 2013), the influence of Fire energy will be overwhelmingly dominant. The regulatory power of the Tri-gathering Principle is on par with a federal bureau.

Figure 101: Earthly Branches Tri-gathering Principle

亥	申	巳	寅
子	酉	午	卯
丑	戌	未	辰
三	三	三	三
會	會	會	會
水	金	火	木
局	局	局	局

YinMaoChenSanHuiMuJü
SiWuWeiSanHuiHuoJü
ShenYouXüSanHuiJinJü
HaiZiChouSanHuiShuiJü

Yin, Mao, and Chen are gathering into the Eastern Wood
Si, Wu, and Wei are gathering into the Southern Fire
Shen, You, and Xü are gathering into the Western Metal
Hai, Zi, and Chou are gathering into the Northern Water

4.9 *DiZhiSanHe* 地支三合
Earthly Branches Tri-combination Principle (Triangle Relationship)

In the Tri-combination Principle, or Triangle Relationship, three Earthly Branches from two or more different directional groups form a tripartite collection, the energy from which transforms into a very strong single Elemental energy. The influence of the Tri-combination Principle is less strong than the Tri-gathering Principle. However, the Elemental effect of a Triangle Relationship Element will be significantly greater on a given situation than a series of repeated, individual Elemental presences. For example, Yin 寅, Wu 午 and Xü 戌 together create the Fire Triangle relationship, with a regulatory power that can be likened to a state bureau, whereas a gathering of two Fire (Southern) Earthly Branches could be likened to a local bureau.

Figure 102: Earthly Branches Tri-combination Principle

申　巳　寅　亥
子　酉　午　卯
辰　丑　戌　未
三　三　三　三
合　合　合　合
水　金　火　木
局　局　局　局

HaiMaoWeiSanHeMuJü
YinWuXüSanHeHuoJü
SiYouChouSanHeJinJü
ShenZiChenSanHeShuiJü

Hai, Mao and Wei combine to Wood
Yin, Wu and Xü combine to Fire
Si, You and Chou combine to Metal
Shen, Zi and Chen combine to Water

4.10 *DiZhiLiuChong* 地支六冲
Earthly Branches Six-Repellings Principle

The following six pairs of Earthly Branches forcefully push each away upon coming together. These pairs lie directly opposite from one another and their energetic relationship is repelling.

Figure 103: Earthly Branches Six-Repellings Principle

巳	辰	卯	寅	丑	子
亥	戌	酉	申	未	午
相	相	相	相	相	相
冲	冲	冲	冲	冲	冲

ZiWuXiangChong
ChouWeiXiangChong
YinShenXiangChong
MaoYouXiangChong
ChenWüXiangChong
SiHaiXiangChong

Zi and Wu repel each other
Chou and Wei repel each other
Yin and Shen repel each other
Mao and You repel each other
Chen and Xü repel each other
Si and Hai repel each other

4.11 *LiuQi* 六氣 Six Cosmological Qi

Similar to *WuYun* 五運 (see Section 4.6), *LiuQi* 六氣 is a Chinese term that specifically refers to the six cosmological transformative energies that occur during the annual energetic cycle according to the yearly Earthly Branch. The *LiuQi* are *Feng* 風—Wind, *Han* 寒—Cold, *Shu* 暑—Heat, *Shi* 濕—Damp, *Zao* 燥—Dry, and *Re* 熱—Hot. These six Qi are the Five Elements manifested in climate patterns: Wind is Wood, Cold is Water, Dry is Metal, Damp is Earth, and Heat and Hot are both Fire (Heat is Ministerial Fire whereas Hot is Imperial Fire). These six Qi are also described as six different types of Yin or Yang energy: Wind—*JueYin* 厥陰 (Reverse Yin), Hot—*ShaoYin* 少陰 (Minor Yin), Damp—*TaiYin* 太陰 (Major Yin), Cold—*TaiYang* 太陽 (Major Yang), Dry—*YangMing* 陽明 (Yang Brightness), and Heat—*ShaoYang* 少陽 (Minor Yang).

The *LiuQi* have two parts, the *ZhuQi* 主氣 (host Qi) and *KeQi* 客氣 (guest Qi). The six energies of the host Qi follow the same order each year: *JueYin* Wind Wood, *ShaoYin* Imperial Fire, *ShaoYang* Ministerial Fire, *TaiYin* Damp Earth, *YangMing* Dry Metal, and *TaiYang* Cold Water. The order of guest Qi changes each year according to the yearly Earthly Branch transformation pattern. Each pair of six repelling Branches (see Section 4.10) has the same guest Qi pattern. Table 7 shows the six host and guest Qi phases of each Branch.

Table 7: Six cosmological transformative energies of the annual cycle

LiuQi 六氣	Earthly Branch	ZhuKe 主客	Six cosmological transformative energies of the annual energetic cycle					
			1st	2nd	3rd	4th	5th	6th
ShaoYin 少陰	**Zi** 子	Host	JueYin 厥陰 Wind Wood	ShaoYin 少陰 Imperial Fire	ShaoYang 少陽 Ministerial Fire	TaiYin 太陰 Damp Earth	YangMing 陽明 Dry Metal	TaiYang 太陽 Cold Water
	Wu 午	Guest	TaiYang 太陽 Cold Water	JueYin 厥陰 Wind Wood	ShaoYin 少陰 Imperial Fire	TaiYin 太陰 Damp Earth	ShaoYang 少陽 Ministerial Fire	YangMing 陽明 Dry Metal
TaiYin 太陰	**Chou** 丑	Host	JueYin 厥陰 Wind Wood	ShaoYin 少陰 Imperial Fire	ShaoYang 少陽 Ministerial Fire	TaiYin 太陰 Damp Earth	YangMing 陽明 Dry Metal	TaiYang 太陽 Cold Water
	Wei 未	Guest	JueYin 厥陰 Wind Wood	ShaoYin 少陰 Imperial Fire	TaiYin 太陰 Damp Earth	ShaoYang 少陽 Ministerial Fire	YangMing 陽明 Dry Metal	TaiYang 太陽 Cold Water
ShaoYang 少陽	**Yin** 寅	Host	JueYin 厥陰 Wind Wood	ShaoYin 少陰 Imperial Fire	ShaoYang 少陽 Ministerial Fire	TaiYin 太陰 Damp Earth	YangMing 陽明 Dry Metal	TaiYang 太陽 Cold Water
	Shen 申	Guest	ShaoYin 少陰 Imperial Fire	TaiYin 太陰 Damp Earth	ShaoYang 少陽 Ministerial Fire	YangMing 陽明 Dry Metal	TaiYang 太陽 Cold Water	JueYin 厥陰 Wind Wood
YangMing 陽明	**Mao** 卯	Host	JueYin 厥陰 Wind Wood	ShaoYin 少陰 Imperial Fire	ShaoYang 少陽 Ministerial Fire	TaiYin 太陰 Damp Earth	YangMing 陽明 Dry Metal	TaiYang 太陽 Cold Water
	You 酉	Guest	TaiYin 太陰 Damp Earth	ShaoYang 少陽 Ministerial Fire	YangMing 陽明 Dry Metal	TaiYang 太陽 Cold Water	JueYin 厥陰 Wind Wood	ShaoYin 少陰 Imperial Fire
TaiYang 太陽	**Chen** 辰	Host	JueYin 厥陰 Wind Wood	ShaoYin 少陰 Imperial Fire	ShaoYang 少陽 Ministerial Fire	TaiYin 太陰 Damp Earth	YangMing 陽明 Dry Metal	TaiYang 太陽 Cold Water
	Xü 戌	Guest	ShaoYang 少陽 Ministerial Fire	YangMing 陽明 Dry Metal	TaiYang 太陽 Cold Water	JueYin 厥陰 Wind Wood	ShaoYin 少陰 Imperial Fire	TaiYin 太陰 Damp Earth
JueYin 厥陰	**Si** 巳	Host	JueYin 厥陰 Wind Wood	ShaoYin 少陰 Imperial Fire	ShaoYang 少陽 Ministerial Fire	TaiYin 太陰 Damp Earth	YangMing 陽明 Dry Metal	TaiYang 太陽 Cold Water
	Hai 亥	Guest	YangMing 陽明 Dry Metal	TaiYang 太陽 Cold Water	JueYin 厥陰 Wind Wood	ShaoYin 少陰 Imperial Fire	TaiYin 太陰 Damp Earth	ShaoYang 少陽 Ministerial Fire

4.12 *DiZhiLiuHai* 地支六害
Earthly Branches Six-Harmings Principle

There are six pairs of Earthly Branches that will damage or cause harm to one another when they meet. We learned in the Earthly Branches Six Unions Principle that the pairs Zi and Chou and Wu 午 and Wei have a special connection with each other. In the Earthly Branches Six-Repellings Principle, we see that the pairs Zi 子 and Wu 午 and Chou 丑 and Wei 未 repel each other. When we keep both of these principles in mind, it makes sense that both Zi 子 and Wei 未 and Chou 丑 and Wu 午 damage each other—each is repelling the special paired partner of the other.

Figure 104: Earthly Branches Six-Harmings Principle

申 酉 卯 寅 丑 子
亥 戌 辰 巳 午 未
相 相 相 相 相 相
害 害 害 害 害 害

ZiWeiXiangHai
ChouWuXiangHai
YinSiXiangHai
MaoChenXiangHai
YouXüXiangHai
ShenHaiXiangHai

Zi and Wei damage each other
Chou and Wu damage each other
Yin and Si damage each other
Mao and Chen damage each other
You and Xü damage each other
Shen and Hai damage each other

4.13 *LiuShiHuaJia* 六十花甲
Sixty Stem Branch Combinations

Although we use the Heavenly Stems and Earthly Branches separately on certain occasions, it is more common to use the combination of one Stem and one Branch as one complete unit. This is especially true with respect to Chinese cosmology and astrology—both complete fields of study and each based on the Chinese calendar.

The most basic rule one must always follow when pairing a Stem and Branch is that the Yang Stems are only coupled with Yang Branches and Yin Stems will only combine with Yin Branches. In this system, the Yin and Yang couplet obey the YinYang numeric order system—even numbers are considered Yin and odd numbers are considered Yang. For example, Jia 甲 is the first Stem and the number one, being an odd number, is Yang. Accordingly, Jia 甲 is Yang and can only combine with one of the six Yang Branches (Zi 子, Yin 寅, Chen 辰, Wu 午, Shen 申, and Xü 戌—remembering the correct order of the Stems and Branches is essential here). There are five Yang Heavenly Stems and six Yang Earthly Branches, which means that there are 30 possible combinations of Yang Stems and Branches. Given that the same is true for Yin Stem/Branch combinations, there is a chronological sequence of 60 total possible Stem–Branch pairs.

Table 8: LiuShiHuaJia 六十花甲 Sexagenary Cycle

1. 甲子 Metal	11. 甲戌 Fire	21. 甲申 Water	31. 甲午 Metal	41. 甲辰 Fire	51. 甲寅 Water
2. 乙丑 Metal	12. 乙亥 Fire	22. 乙酉 Water	32. 乙未 Metal	42. 乙巳 Fire	52. 乙卯 Water
3. 丙寅 Fire	13. 丙子 Water	23. 丙戌 Earth	33. 丙申 Fire	43. 丙午 Water	53. 丙辰 Earth
4. 丁卯 Fire	14. 丁丑 Water	24. 丁亥 Earth	34. 丁酉 Fire	44. 丁未 Water	54. 丁巳 Earth
5. 戊辰 Wood	15. 戊寅 Earth	25. 戊子 Fire	35. 戊戌 Wood	45. 戊申 Earth	55. 戊午 Fire
6. 己巳 Wood	16. 己卯 Earth	26. 己丑 Fire	36. 己亥 Wood	46. 己酉 Earth	56. 己未 Fire
7. 庚午 Earth	17. 庚辰 Metal	27. 庚寅 Wood	37. 庚子 Earth	47. 庚戌 Metal	57. 庚申 Wood
8. 辛未 Earth	18. 辛巳 Metal	28. 辛卯 Wood	38. 辛丑 Earth	48. 辛亥 Metal	58. 辛酉 Wood
9. 壬申 Metal	19. 壬午 Wood	29. 壬辰 Water	39. 壬寅 Metal	49. 壬子 Wood	59. 壬戌 Water
10. 癸酉 Metal	20. 癸未 Wood	30. 癸巳 Water	40. 癸卯 Metal	50. 癸丑 Wood	60. 癸亥 Water

Traditionally, these 60 units are assigned a numeric order. The first unit is JiaZi 甲子, which combines the first Heavenly Stem (Jia 甲) with the first Earthly Branch (Zi 子). The second unit, YiChou 乙丑, combines the second Stem with the second Branch, and so on, each creating its own Five Element nature. This newly created Five Elements nature is called *NaYinWuXing* 納音五行 —musicalized Five Elements—because it is based on the classical Chinese musical scales. After all 60 pairs have been generated, the cycle repeats itself. The Chinese name for this sexagenary cycle is *LiuShiHuaJia* 六十花甲 (Sixty Transforms [back to] Jia). The oracle bones of the Shang Dynasty show that this sexagenary cycle has been in use for recording time in daily increments since the 2nd century BCE, and is still the traditional method of numbering days and years in the Chinese lunisolar calendar.

千古精神

癸巳仲夏吉日
乾元之子 於瑞典

5

GanZhi JingShen 干支精神

The Spirit of the GanZhi

As discussed in previous chapters, *TianGan* (the ten Heavenly Stems) represent the ten organ systems of the body and *DiZhi* (the twelve Earthly Branches) represent the twelve main meridian systems. In traditional Chinese philosophy, the body is likened to a great nation with ten majestic cities (the ten organ systems), which are connected by twelve pathways of complex communications and exchange—a combination of railroads, highways, waterways, electricity, telecommunications and digital information all rolled into one (the twelve meridian systems). The quality of each Stem, its propensity for alchemical transformation and its relationships with other Stems and Branches provides extraordinary insight into understanding pathology and physiology of our physical body, the inner workings of our emotional realm and our potential for spiritual development.

In order to help advanced practitioners connect to the spirit of the GanZhi, we will share ten celebrated poems from the Chinese astrology classic, *DiTianShui* 滴天髓, written by the Song Dynasty Yijing Master, JingTu 京圖. By offering our interpretation of these poems, we hope you will grasp the centrally important Five Element relationships between each Stem and the individual Elements. In traditional Chinese medicine, Chinese astrology is an advanced method of diagnosis. In the astrology chart, the Stem of the individual's day of birth represents his or her self. Having the ability to correctly interpret the character of the birth day Stem, its alchemical transformation properties, and Five Element relationships with the other Stems and Branches in the birth chart is a way to read definitive life patterns, diagnose his or her strengths and weakness, and understand the cosmological influences on the individual at any given time throughout all stages of life. To distill the GanZhi to its essence is a way to access the heart of all the information they provide.

Again, this chapter is not intended to be a beginner's text; please take your time to review the previous chapters and other related fundamental material (for example, the *HuangDiNeiJing* 黃帝內經, *ShangHanLun* 傷寒論, *NanJing* 難經, *HuangTingJing* 黃庭經, etc.) if you find understanding these poems challenging.

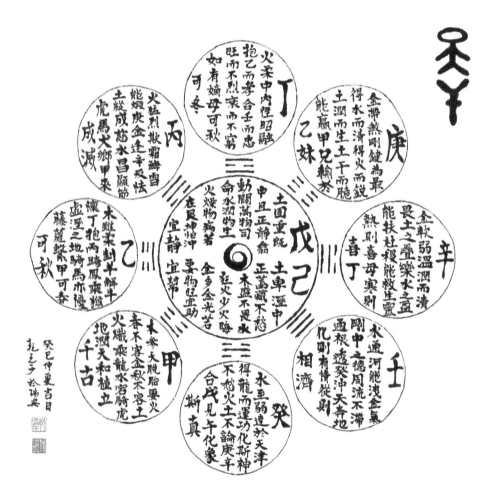

Figure 105: Ten celebrated TianGan poems, written by Song Dynasty Yijing Master JingTu 京圖

甲

木參天脫胎要火
春不容金秋不容土
火熾乘龍水宕騎虎
地潤天和植立千古

5.1 JiaMu 甲木

We can extract the fundamental symbolic meaning of Jia and the other Heavenly Stems from the *DiTianShui* 滴天髓. We will present Master Jing's poems in the traditional way—top to bottom, right to left.

植 地 水 火 秋 春 脫 甲
立 潤 宕 熾 不 不 胎 木
千 天 騎 乘 容 容 要 參
古 和 虎 龍 土 金 火 天

JiaMuCanTian

TuoTaiYaoHuo
ChunBuRongJin QiuBuRongTu
HuoChiChengLong ShuiDangQiHu

DiRunTianHe
ZhiLiQianGu

Jia Wood stretches skyward

Brought forth by Fire
Springtime refuses Metal, Autumn exhausts Earth
Afire riding Dragon, Bestriding Tiger through torrents

Harmonized by Heaven and Earth
Jia stands 1,000 years

Commentary

JiaMuCanTian 甲木參天

Jia Wood stretches skyward

Yang Wood (Jia) has powerful, initiating, surging and penetrating life energy, like a sprout breaking through the earth and a tree boldly growing towards heaven.

TuoTaiYaoHuo 脫胎要火

Brought forth by Fire

Wood gives birth to Fire, and Fire is needed to illuminate the command of Wood. As the early springtime plants need the increasing light and warmth of the sun to flourish, Jia prospers when Fire is present to balance it. For example, if Jia is the master stem in your Chinese astrological chart, you will feel vibrant during the Fire season and around fiery people, and people will be drawn towards you when you wear red. Within the body, Jia also represents the gallbladder. If you are working towards strengthening the function of the gallbladder, utilizing Fire (like the Fire points on the gallbladder channel or including specific Fire herbs in your formula) will be very helpful.

ChunBuRongJin 春不容金

Springtime refuses Metal

In general, by rule of the Five Elements controlling principle, Metal controls the Wood. However, spring is the season of the Wood Element and is the reigning period of Jia. During the spring season Jia is in its full glory and during this time of extreme strength it will reverse-control Metal.

QiuBuRongTu 秋不容土

Autumn exhausts Earth

Earth gives birth to Metal and thus the Metal Element can drain energy from Earth. Autumn is the season of Metal. During the autumn season Metal gains strength and further drains the Earth Element. Remember that Wood controls and potentially weakens Earth. During the autumn season, the presence of strong Jia Wood will further weaken the Earth energy. For example, if a day Stem Jia person is born in autumn Metal season, this person will likely be susceptible to chronic digestion issues due to the weakening influence of Jia and Metal on spleen and stomach Earth.

HuoChiChengLong 火熾乘龍

Afire riding Dragon

The Dragon in this line refers to the Earthly Branch Chen 辰. Chen is itself an Earth Element and is also the reservoir of the Water Element. According to the control principle, Wood controls and thus can weaken Earth energy. However, when strong Fire Element is represented, the Fire will help balance the controlling effects of Jia Wood on Chen Earth.

How is that possible? Instead of exerting energy through controlling Earth, Jia Wood can instead channel its resources towards nurturing Fire. Fire gives birth to Earth. Strong fire, supported by Jia Wood, will support and strengthen Earth. Do you remember the hidden Water Element within Chen? This hidden Water helps temper the Fire so that Fire will not overwhelm and scorch Earth. In these circumstances, Jia Wood and Chen Earth achieve the union and fluidity of complete cooperation.

ShuiDangQiHu 水宕騎虎

Bestriding Tiger through torrents

In this verse, the Tiger refers to the Earthly Branch Yin 寅 Wood. Yin 寅 is the root of Jia and brings Jia Wood strength. According to the Five Elements creation principle, Water gives birth to and nourishes Wood. However, very strong Water can deluge weak Wood. When Jia Wood and Yin Tiger are found rooted together (e.g. the Stem and Branch combination *JiaYin* 甲寅), there is no concern of being overcome by strong Water.

DiRunTianHe 地潤天和

Harmonized by Heaven and Earth

Harmony in the heavens and moisture on the earth describes a general state of overall balance. In this case it also represents a balance between and among the Heavenly Stems and Earthly Branches of the astrology chart.

ZhiLiQianGu 植立千古

Jia stands 1,000 years

If Jia Wood is well supported by the other Stems and Branches as suggested in the previous line, it will gain lasting strength and power.

乙

木雖柔刲羊解牛
懷丁抱丙跨鳳乘猴
虛溼之地騎馬亦慢
藤蘿繫甲可春

可秋

丁

火柔中內性昭融
抱乙而孝合壬而忠
旺而不烈衰而不窮
如有嫡母可秋可冬

丙

火猛烈欺霜侮雪
能煆庚金逢辛反怯
土眾成慈水猖顯節
木雖未刲羊解牛

乙妹

得水而清得火而銳
土潤而生土干而脆
能贏甲兄輸壬

甲

木參天脫胎要火
春不容金秋不容土
火熾乘龍水宕騎虎
地潤天和植立
斯真

癸

水至弱達於天津
得龍而運功化斯
不愁火土不論庚
合戊見午化象

剛中之德周流不滯
通根透癸沖天奔地
化則有情從則
相濟

5.2 YiMu 乙木

可　藤　騎　虛　跨　懷　剖　乙
春　羅　馬　濕　鳳　丁　羊　木
可　繫　亦　之　乘　抱　解　雖
秋　甲　慢　地　猴　丙　牛　柔

YiMuSuiRou
KuiYangJieNiu
HuaiDingBaoBing KuaFengChengHou
XüShiZhiDi QiMaYiYou
TengLuoJiJia KeChunKeQiu

Gentle Yi Wood
Beheads Goat and butchers Ox

Embosomed by Ding and Bing
Glides with Phoenix and swings with Monkey

In the marshlands
Even the horseman is troubled

A vine clinging to a tree
Grows in spring and fall

Commentary

YiMuSuiRou 乙木雖柔

Gentle Yi Wood

Yi (Yin Wood) represents early growth with bendable, twisting branches that maneuver around obstacles. Yi's power lies in its gentle flexibility. The energy of Yi is just like the strong life energy of grasses, weeds, vines, and twisted trees, which readily contort themselves, working through rocks and other impediments to find a way to keep growing.

KuiYangJieNiu 剖羊解牛

Beheads Goat and butchers Ox

Don't be fooled by Yi's soft nature—there is forceful energy hidden within. Goat is the animal sign for the Earthly Branch Wei 未 and Ox is representative of Chou 丑. Both Wei and Chou belong to the Earth Element. The gentle strength of Yi Wood can overpower Earth energy.

HuaiDingBaoBing 懷丁抱丙

Embosomed by Ding and Bing

Ding is Yin Fire and Bing is Yang Fire, and together they represent all Fire energy—the summer season, southern areas, hot environments, red colors, etc. This line of the poem links with the next sentence to complete the meaning.

KuaFengChengHou 跨鳳乘猴

Glides with Phoenix and swings with Monkey

The Phoenix and Monkey are the spiritual animals of the Earthly Branches You 酉 and Shen 申. Both You and Shen are of the Metal Element. In Five Elements control cycle, Metal controls the Wood. However, if Yi Wood is well supported and embraced by Fire, it will be able to reverse-control Metal.

XüShiZhiDi 虛濕之地

In the marshlands

The hollow and damp earth in this verse paints the picture of Earth inundated with Water.

QiMaYiYou 騎馬亦憂

Even the horseman is troubled

These two lines are also interpreted together. The Horse is the spiritual animal of Earthly Branch Wu 午 Fire, and is used here to represent the Fire Element. In this situation, although Yi can be strengthened by the presence of Fire, when there is an overabundance of Water, Wood will become uprooted. Whilst Water typically nurtures Wood, excessive amounts will have a damaging, flood-like effect. You may be able to recall an instance where you have seen this pattern in nature or in your clinical practice.

TengLuoJiJia 藤羅繫甲

A vine clinging to a tree

Jia (Yang Wood—here, the tree) serves as an anchoring support for *Luo*, the flexible vine (Yi or Yin Wood).

KeChunKeQiu 可春可秋

Grows in spring and fall

We interpret these last two lines as a couplet as well. In classical Chinese literature, the words spring and autumn are used together to refer to an entire yearly cycle. Here, Master JingTu is telling us that Yi Wood can flourish in all seasons as long as it receives the support of Jia Yang Wood.

丙

火猛烈欺霜雪
能煅庚金逢辛反怯
土縱成慈水昌顯節
虎馬犬鄉甲來
成滅

5.3 BingHuo 丙火

甲　虎　水　土　逢　能　欺　丙
來　馬　昌　縱　辛　煅　霜　火
成　犬　顯　成　反　庚　侮　猛
滅　鄉　節　慈　怯　金　雪　烈

BingHuoMengLie
QiShuangWuXue
NengDuanGengJin FengXinFanQie
TuZongChengCi ShuiChangXianJie
HuMaQuanXiang JiaLaiChengMie

Bing Fire blazes fiercely

Bullying frost, humiliating snow
Smelts Geng Metal
Fears Xin Metal
Abundant Earth, abounding compassion
Wild Water instills loyalty

In Tiger, Horse, and Dog's village
Even Jia becomes ash

Commentary

BingHuoMengLie 丙火猛烈

Bing Fire blazes fiercely

Of all the ten Heavenly Stems, Bing has the most powerful Yang energy.

QiShuangWuXue 欺霜侮雪

Bullying frost, humiliating snow

Here, frost and snow refer to the presence of a strong Water Element. Typically, Water controls Fire. However, Bing Fire is blazing and has the ability to reverse control Water.

NengDuanGengJin 能煅庚金

Smelts Geng Metal

Although the Heavenly Stem Geng 庚 exerts formidable Yang Metal energy influence on any given situation, Bing Fire is able to effectively control it.

FengXinFanQie 逢辛反怯

Fears Xin Metal

In the Five Elements alchemical process, Yang Fire Bing and Yin Metal Xin interact with each other in such a way that they transform to Water energy. When Bing and Xin are present together, Bing can be completely extinguished by the transformed Water.

TuZongChengCi 土縱成慈

Abundant Earth, abounding compassion

Earth is the child of Fire. A strong Earth influence will help draw the intensity of Bing's Yang Fire, allowing Fire to channel its burning energy towards nurturing its child.

ShuiChangXianJie 水昌顯節

Wild Water instills loyalty

Water controls Fire and strong Water will dampen any common Fire. Bing Fire, however, is not your typical Fire—its function is actually enhanced by the presence of strong Water. This is because Water of equal force is able to refine Bing Fire, keeping it aligned with the wisdom of Water.

HuMaQuanXiang 虎馬犬鄉

In Tiger, Horse, and Dog's village

Tiger, Horse, and Dog are representations of the Earthly Branches Yin 寅, Wu 午, and Xü 戌, which together form the tri-combination "gang" of Fire (see Section 4.9). Bing Fire, the leader of the gang of Fire, is unstoppable around Tiger, Horse, and Dog.

JiaLaiChengMie 甲來成滅

Even Jia becomes ash

As discussed in Section 5.1, Jia typically flourishes in the presence of Fire. However, even the power of great Yang Wood Jia will be totally overcome in the face of Bing Fire and the Fire gang.

丁

火柔中內性昭融
抱乙而孝合壬而忠
旺而不烈衰而不窮
如有嫡母可秋
可冬

5.4 DingHuo 丁火

丁火柔中
內性昭融
抱乙而孝
合壬而忠
旺而不烈
衰而不窮
如有嫡母
可秋可冬

DingHuoRouZhong
NeiXingZhaoRong
BaoYiErXiao HeRenErZhong
WangErBuLie ShuaiErBuQiong
RuYouDiMu KeQiuKeDong

Ding Fire, gentle within
Inner character bright and earnest

Embraces Yi with piety,
Devoted to Ren

Blazing but not dangerous
Diminishes without dying out

With its blood mother
Peaceful in autumn and winter

Commentary

DingHuoRouZhong 丁火柔中

Ding Fire, gentle within

The quality of Yin Fire is soft and feels warm and comfortable.

NeiXingZhaoRong 內性昭融

Inner character bright and earnest

Ding Fire qualities also include virtuous, openheartedness, and charitable.

BaoYiErXiao 抱乙而孝

Embraces Yi with piety

Typically, in the Five Element parent–child relationship (see Section 4.1), the "child" element will drain some amount of energy from the "parent" element. However, Yi Yin Wood has a special relationship to Ding Yin Fire—one that is similar to that of a kind step-mother or doting nanny. If there is a situation in which Yi Wood is together with Ding Fire, Ding's gentle fire will warm up the Wood and support its function, as opposed to draining Wood's energy.

HeRenErZhong 合壬而忠

Devoted to Ren

In general, Fire and Water oppose each other. An exception to this general rule is found in the case of Ding Yin Fire and Ren Yang Water. When these two come together, they may transform into the Wood Element. The Wood Element feeds Fire.

WangErBuLie 旺而不烈

Blazing but not dangerous

It is possible for Ding Yin Fire to have a very strong energy without resorting to burning its surroundings. A strong Ding person, for example, could become an exceptional leader—very powerful yet not overbearing.

ShuaiErBuQiong 衰而不窮

Diminishes without dying out

Ding Yin Fire energy is gentle, consistent, and enduring.

RuYouDiMu 如有嫡母

With its blood mother

The blood mother of Ding is Jia Yang Wood. This line continues with the next:

KeQiuKeDong 可秋可冬

Peaceful in autumn and winter

Autumn is the Metal season and winter is the Water season, and according to the Five Element creation and control relationships, both Metal and Water typically deplete Fire. However, when Ding Fire is supported by its mother element, Jia Wood, it can maintain its strength in environments dominated by either Metal or Water.

戊　己

土面重畏　中且正靜翕　動闢萬物司　命水潤物生　火燥物病若　在艮坤怕沖　宜靜宜幫

土車逕中　正藏萬藏不愁　木盛不畏水　狂火少火晦　金多金光若　要物旺宜助

丁　丙　甲　癸

5.5 WuTu 戊土

怕　若　火　水　萬　靜　既　戊
沖　在　燥　潤　物　翕　中　土
宜　艮　物　物　司　動　且　固
靜　坤　病　生　命　辟　正　重

WuTuGuZhong
JiZhongQieZheng
JingXiDongPi WanWuShiMing
ShuiRunWuSheng HuoZaoWuBing
RuoZaiGenKun PaChongYiJing

Wu Earth—solid and heavy
Centered and upright

Still and closed, moving and open
Commands Ten-Thousand-Things

When nourished by Water, life flows
When parched by Fire, illness follows

Combined with *Gen* or *Kun*
Pushed around if unstable

Commentary

WuTuGuZhong 戊土固重

Wu Earth—solid and heavy

Solid and heavy describes the natural character of Wu 午 Yang Earth.

JiZhongQieZheng 既中且正

Centered and upright

Yang Earth is stable, centered, and honorable.

JingXiDongPi 靜翕動闢

Still and closed, moving and open

Closed here is used to represent the Yin tranquil state, whereas open refers to the Yang activity state. The solidity of Yang Earth expresses itself somewhere along the continuum between admirable dedication and frustrating stubbornness. Yang Earth is difficult to change once it has set its course—it can be unmovable in some situations and unstoppable in others.

WanWuShiMing 萬物司命

Commands Ten-Thousand-Things

Yang Earth has the power to support or destroy everything in existence.

ShuiRunWuSheng 水潤物生

When nourished by Water, life flows

Wu 午 Yang Earth needs nourishment from Water in order to bring forth its vibrancy.

HuoZaoWuBing 火燥物病

When parched by Fire, illness follows

Fire dries up Yang Earth to the point of deprivation.

RuoZaiGenKun 若在艮坤

Combined with Gen or Kun

In Chinese astrology, the trigram *Gen* is sometimes used to represent the Earthly Branch Yin 寅, which is the Yang Wood Branch, while the trigram *Kun* is sometimes used to represent the Earthly Branch *Shen* 申, which is Yang Metal. This verse, completed by the following line, tells us what to expect if Wu 戊 is paired with Yin or Shen.

PaChongYiJing 怕沖宜靜

Pushed around if unstable

Wood controls Earth, Earth gives birth to Metal. When Wu 戊 is paired with Yin or Shen it becomes unstable and lacking a strong rootedness. In this circumstance, unless Wu Yang Earth is anchored by other supporting elements, it will crumble.

戊　己

戊己

土固重既
土車溼中

中且正靜翕
正萬藏不愁

動闢萬物司
木盛不畏水

命水潤物生
莊火少火晦

火燥物病若
金多金光若

在艮坤怕沖
要物旺宜助

宜靜宜幫

丁

丙

甲

癸

得水而清得火而銳
能贏甲兄輸乙妹
土潤而生土午而脆
抱乙而孝合壬而冬
如有嬌母可冬
火來中內旺昭融

能燃庚金至于夭怯
火盆烈欺霜酶曰
土從戍苟水昌顯勛
木唯來剋牛辭牛

火熾乘龍水宏騎虎
春不容金秋不容土
荷天脫胎要火
龍而運功化斯
愁火土不論庚
水主弱逢於天津
合戍見午化
斯真

剛中之德周流不滯
通根透癸沖天奔地
斯有情從則
相濟

5.6 JiTu 己土

己土畀濕
中正蓄藏
不愁木勝
不畏水狂
火少火晦
金多金光
若要物旺
宜助宜幫

JiTuBiShi
ZhongZhengXüCang
BuChouMuSheng BuWeiShuiKuang
HuoShaoHuoHui JinDuoJinGuang
RuYaoWuWang YiZhuYiBang

Ji Earth, humble and damp
Centered, righteous, holding within

Comfortable with strong Wood
Undaunted by powerful Water
Small Fire is dimmed
Many Metals shine

For all things to prosper
Support Ji Earth

Commentary

JiTuBiShi 己土畀濕

Ji Earth, humble and damp

Yin Earth is moist, fertile and accepting—all qualities that allow things to grow.

ZhongZhengXüCang 中正蓄藏

Centered, righteous, holding within

Yin Earth is grounded, virtuous, receptive, and modest.

BuChouMuSheng 不愁木勝

Comfortable with strong Wood

According to the Five Elements' creation/control relationships, Wood controls Earth. This being so, we would expect strong Wood to weaken Earth. However, the receptive quality of Yin Earth draws Wood in and allows it to root, making it possible for Ji to stay balanced even in the presence of abundant Wood.

BuWeiShuiKuang 不畏水狂

Undaunted by powerful Water

In general, strong Water will exert reverse-control on Earth and thus leave it weakened. However, because Ji Earth is able to absorb excess Water, it does not get washed away.

HuoShaoHuoHui 火少火晦

Small Fire is dimmed

Typically, Earth will sap resources from Fire. This is especially true when a strong Ji Earth feeds off an already weak Fire.

JinDuoJinGuang 金多金光

Many Metals shine

We would expect Metal to deplete Earth. However, Ji Earth is damp and generous and even in the presence of many Metal Elements, Ji Earth provides without being exhausted. With this steady flow of nourishment, Metal shines!

RuYaoWuWang 若要物旺

For all things to prosper

This verse is considered complete with the line that follows:

YiZhuYiBang 宜助宜幫

Support Ji Earth

Yin Earth is the quintessential mother, providing for and sustaining everything. In order to maintain this nurturing quality, Ji itself must be supported, especially by the presence of Fire and other Earth Elements.

庚

金帶煞剛鍵為最

得水而清得火而銳

土潤而生土干而脆

能贏甲兄輸癸

乙妹

5.7 GengJin 庚金

輸 能 土 土 得 得 剛 庚
於 贏 干 潤 火 水 鍵 金
乙 甲 而 而 而 而 為 帶
妹 兄 脆 生 銳 清 最 煞

GengJinDaiSha
GangJianWeiZui
DeShuiErQing DeHuoErRui
TuRunErSheng TuGanErCui
NengYingJiaXiong ShuYuYiMei

Geng Metal has martial power
Unrivaled strength and mastery

With Water shines pure
Fire hones sharp
Moist Earth brings life
Dry Earth shatters

Triumphs over elder brother (Jia)
Subdued by younger sister (Yi)

Commentary

GengJinDaiSha 庚金帶煞

Geng Metal has martial power

Yang Metal has powerful warrior energy.

GangJianWeiZui 剛鍵為最

Unrivaled strength and mastery

The impressive strength and mastery of a Geng Metal person may make them a renowned general, fighter, judge, financial officer, surgeon, or musician.

DeShuiErQing 得水而清

With Water shines pure

Metal gives birth to Water and Water shows off the talent of Metal. *Qing* 清 means pure, flawless, and clear, and is used in Chinese literature to describe the highest quality of metal. This verse shows us that the elegance and genius of Geng Metal shines forth with the influence of Water.

DeHuoErRui 得火而銳

Fire hones sharp

"Sharp" represents the clean, cutting function of Metal. Fire refines Metal, honing the spiritual sword to cut through material attachments.

TuRunErSheng 土潤而生

Moist Earth brings life

Moist Earth refers to Yin Earth, which nourishes dry Yang Metal.

TuGanErCui 土干而脆

Dry Earth shatters

Dry Earth describes Yang Earth, which causes trouble on Yang Metal.

NengYingJiaXiong 能赢甲兄

Triumphs over elder brother (Jia)

Once Geng Yang Metal and Jia Yang Wood come together, Geng will control and weaken Jia.

ShuYuYiMei 輸於乙妹

Subdued by younger sister (Yi)

However, when Geng Yang Metal meets Yi Yin Wood, there is no conflict between them. According to the Five Elements alchemical transformation principle, Geng and Yi combine together to become one Metal family.

辛

金軟弱溫潤而清　畏土之疊藥水之盈　能扶社稷能救生靈　熱則喜母寒則喜丁

5.8 XinJin 辛金

寒　熱　能　能　樂　畏　溫　辛
則　則　救　扶　水　土　潤　金
喜　喜　生　社　之　之　而　軟
丁　母　靈　稷　盈　疊　清　弱

XinJinRuanRou
WengRunErQing
WeiTuZhiDie LeShuiZhiYing
NengFuSheJi NengJiuShengLing
ReZheXiMu HanZheXiDing

Xin Metal: soft and delicate
Warm, moist, and pure

Afraid of heavy Earth
Delights in abundant Water

Supports the King
Saving all beings

In heat it loves mother
In cold it loves Ding Fire

Commentary

XinJinRuanRou 辛金軟弱

Xin Metal: soft and delicate

Xin Metal is gentle and flexible, as opposed to the hard and rigid qualities associated with Geng Yang Metal.

WengRunErQing 溫潤而清

Warm, moist, and pure

The character of Xin Yin Metal is warm, moist, pure, and tender.

WeiTuZhiDie 畏土之疊

Afraid of heavy Earth

Heavy Earth will bury the Xin Metal—in other words, Xin Metal will not function well when surrounded by many Earth Element energies.

LeShuiZhiYing 樂水之盈

Delights in abundant Water

Water shows off the talent of Metal and Xin Metal thrives in the presence of water.

NengFuSheJi 能扶社稷

Supports the King

Bing Yang Fire is the King of Xin. The powerful Yang Fire energy tapers when it meets Xin because Xin and Bing can potentially transform into the Water Element.

NengJiuShengLing 能救生靈

Saves all beings

All beings represent the life energy of the Wood Element. Xin Metal is able to transform to Water, which then gives birth to and nourishes all life energy.

ReZheXiMu 熱則喜母

In heat it loves mother

Earth Element is the mother of Xin Metal. Strong Fire can damage Xin Metal unless Xin is protected and supported by Earth. This is because Earth will simultaneously absorb Fire and feed Metal. If Xin Metal represents the day Stem in a person's astrological chart and that person was born in the hot summer (during a period of strong Fire Element energy) and also has Earth Elements in the same chart, he or she is destined to move smoothly through life.

HanZheXiDing 寒則喜丁

In cold it loves Ding Fire

Cold is one of the energy patterns of the Water Element. When the Water Element is overly strong, Xin will need the support of Yin Fire Ding to function properly.

壬

水通河能洩金氣
剛中之德周流不滯
通根透癸沖天奔地
化則有情從則相濟

5.9 RenShui 壬水

從　化　沖　通　周　剛　能　壬
則　則　天　根　流　中　洩　水
相　有　奔　透　不　之　金　通
濟　情　地　癸　滯　德　氣　河

RenShuiTongHe
NengXieJinQi
GangZhongZhiDe ZhouLiuBuZhi
TongGenTouGui ChongTianBenDi
HuaZeYouQing CongZeXiangJi

Ren Water connects to the River
Draining Metal's Qi

Its virtue is tenacity
Coursing without stagnation

Rooted with Gui
Soars through heaven, cascades over earth

Transformation begets humanity
Obeying creates mutuality

Commentary

RenShuiTongHe 壬水通河

Ren Water connects to the River

The River here means the Milky Way. In Chinese tradition, we refer to our galaxy as the Heavenly River. In our creation stories, Heaven first gave birth to Water, making it the first Element created on our planet. With the Heavenly River as its source, Ren Water will never run dry.

NengXieJinQi 能洩金氣

Draining Metal's Qi

Ren Yang Water's strong influence can mellow the intense energy of Metal.

GangZhongZhiDe 剛中之德

Its virtue is tenacity

The Chinese word *De* 德 means virtue and it also carries the meaning of function, quality, and character. Although on the surface Yang Water appears soft and supple, its inner nature is relentless.

ZhouLiuBuZhi 周流不滯

Coursing without stagnation

Ren Yang Water's capacity for continuous circulation is reflected in the natural water cycle (evaporation → condensation → precipitation → groundwater → evaporation → ad infinitum)—the ceaseless movement of water on, above, and below the surface of the Earth.

TongGenTouGui 通根透癸

Rooted with Gui

The next two lines are interpreted together. The root of Ren lies in the Water Element Earthly Branches, Hai and Zi. If ever Ren is paired with either root and Gui is also present…

ChongTianBenDi 沖天奔地

Soars through heaven, cascades over earth

…then Ren Yang Water will become an indomitable force.

HuaZeYouQing 化則有情

Transformation begets humanity

Tireless Ren Yang Water can wash away Wood and Ding Yin Fire can burn the Wood to ash. However, when Ding Fire and Ren Water meet they can transform into Wood. With this transformation, Ren's virtue is channeled into limitless compassion for all life energy (Wood).

CongZeXiangJi 從則相濟

Obeying creates mutuality

Earth is the commander of Water. When Water and Earth are equally matched, Water is able to flow with the controlling energy of Earth as opposed to rising against it. If there is no conflict between Ren Yang Water and the Earth Element, the relationship becomes mutually supportive: Ren Water will nourish the Earth and Earth will carry the Water.

水至弱達於天津
得龍而運功化斯神
不愁火土不論庚辛
合戊見午化象
斯真
癸

能贏甲兄輸乙妹
土潤而生土干而脆
得木而清得火而銳
丁
如有嫡母可秋可冬
旺而不烈衰而不窮
抱乙而孝合壬而忠
火柔中內性昭融

乙妹

剛中之德周流不滯
通根透癸沖天奔地
相濟

丙
能煆庚金逢辛反怯
土從成慈水昌顯節
火協烈欺霜侮雪

木雖柔刲羊解牛

甲
火熾乘龍水宕騎虎
春不容金秋不容土
地潤天和植立

合戊見午化象
不愁火土不論庚辛
得龍而運功化斯神
水至弱達於天津
斯真

合戊見午化象
不愁火土不論庚辛
得龍而運功化斯神
斯真

5.10 GuiShui 癸水

癸水至弱
達於天津
得龍而運 功化斯神
不愁火土 不論庚辛
合戊見午 化象斯真

GuiShuiZhiRuo
DaYuTianJin
DeLongErYun GongHuaSiShen
BuChouHuoTu BuLunGengXin
HeWuXianWu HuaXiangSiZhen

Gui Water, epitome of softness
Reaches the Heavenly Harbor

Free flowing with Dragon
Actualized spiritual transformation

Comfortable with Fire and Earth
Easy around Geng and Xin

When Wu 戊 and Wu 午 appear
The transformation is true!

Commentary

GuiShuiZhiRuo 癸水至弱

Gui Water, epitome of softness

Of all the Heavenly Stems, Gui has the gentlest nature.

DaYuTianJin 達於天津

Reaches the Heavenly Harbor

The Chinese asterism *TianJin* has nine stars and is located within the Western constellation Cygnus. It belongs to the *Nü* 女 region of the 28 Lunar Mansions. *TianJin* is the Heavenly Harbor of the Heavenly River—the Milky Way. Gui Yin Water comes from heaven and its source is endless.

DeLongErYun 得龍而運

Free flowing with Dragon

The dragon here represents the Earthly Branch Chen. Chen is the reservoir of the Water Element and it is also the commander of Gui. In general, Gui Yin Water flows smoothly when accompanied by Chen.

GongHuaSiShen 功化斯神

Actualized spiritual transformation

Gui Yin Water alchemically transforms only in the presence of Chen Dragon. One of the most fundamental and basic principles of Chinese astrology is *FengChenZeHua* 逢辰則化—once Dragon appears, transformation occurs. With the help of Dragon Gui Water may transform to true Fire (spirit).

BuChouHuoTu 不愁火土

Comfortable with Fire and Earth

Strong Fire may reverse control Water and strong Earth may over control Water. However, neither intense Fire nor oppressive Earth can weaken Gui Yin Water, for its Yin power lies untouchable, deep within.

BuLunGengXin 不論庚辛

Easy around Geng and Xin

According to Five Element generating principle, Metal is the parent of Water. Although the parent element typically supports the child element, there are times when the parent is overwhelmingly strong and "over-parents" or harms the child. Gui Yin Water's receptivity allows it to absorb all energy from Xin Yin Metal and Geng Yang Metal, no matter how domineering they may be.

HeWuXianWu 合戊見午

When Wu 戊 and Wu 午 appear

When Heavenly Stem Wu 戊 is partnered with Gui Yin Water and the Earthly Branch Wu 午 is also present…

HuaXiangSiZhen 化象斯真

The transformation is true!

…Gui Yin Water will be completely transformed to Fire. These last two lines relay further conditions needed for true transformation of Gui Water to occur.

運化全乎心　　宇宙立於手

*The Universe is within my hand
and is manifested through my heart.*

坤　剝　觀　否　遯　姤　乾　夬　大壯　泰　臨　復
Kun　Bo　Guan　Pi　Dun　Gou　Qian　Guai　Dazhuang　Tai　Lin　Fu

The Wave of Life

Figure 106: The Wave of Life Diagram (from The 12 Chinese Animals)
The twelve hexagram positions on the fingers represent the Earthly Way of the twelve Earthly Branches. The thumb symbolizes the Heavenly Way of the ten Heavenly Stems. Traditionally, we use these positions on our hand as a tool for calculating Chinese astrological charts and cosmological patterns as well as for healing mudras in internal alchemy practices.

Afterword

In the Daoist tradition, true knowledge pivots around bodily experience, not erudite pursuits. One gains greatest understanding of the ancient wisdom traditions through a burning commitment to inner cultivation practices and by observing the way of nature, often far outside the realm of any formal education system.

After you read through this book, you may still feel as though you are struggling with truly understanding the GanZhi. This is actually a common phenomenon for most of us who embark on the journey to learn this ancient system. When we first started learning about TianGan DiZhi and how they inform the practices of Chinese astrology, cosmology, internal alchemy, and *ZiWu LiuZhu* 子午流注 acupuncture, for example, it was a mind-bending challenge simply to memorize all the meanings of the Stems and Branches, much less get a firm grasp on the knowledge hidden within them. Through years of daily cultivation our studies have blossomed with comprehension and understanding. We hope you can make a commitment to your own inner cultivation practice and allow it to help integrate the information we have presented in this book into the fabric of your heart-mind.

This is not a one-time-read-through book. Rather, it is a reference guide to help you build the foundation for a lifetime of study of ancient Chinese wisdom traditions. To master an art is like creating a delicious, healthy meal (or savoring a nice cup of tea); you must have patience to find the right recipe, search for the best ingredients and put your heart into preparing it well. The process and outcome is quite different to going through the drive-through for some fast food!

We hope the ancient wisdom of the GanZhi will help you reap the bounty of the Great Dao.

Harmonious Qi,

Master Zhongxian Wu and Dr. Karin Taylor Wu
The Yin Water Snake Year, early autumn
Sjögull, Stockholm's archipelago, Sweden

吳氏五行化圖

火

木　　土　　金

水

Appendix

Reference Table 1:
Dynasties of China

Year	Dynasty		
2100–1600 BCE	**Xia** 夏		
1600–1046 BCE	**Shang** 商		
1045–256 BCE	**Zhou** 周	Western Zhou 西周	
		Eastern Zhou 東周	Spring and Autumn 春秋
			Warring State 戰國
221–206 BCE	**Qin** 秦		
206 BCE–220 CE	**Han** 漢	Western Han 西漢	
		Xin 新	
		Eastern Han 東漢	
220–280 CE	**SanGuo** 三國 (Wei 魏, Shu 屬 and Wu 吳)		
265–420 CE	**Jin** 晉	Western Jin 西晉	
		Eastern Jin 東晉	
420–589 CE	**NanBeiChao** 南北朝		
581–618 CE	**Sui** 隋		
618–907 CE	**Tang** 唐	Wu Zhou 武周	
907–1125 CE	**Liao** 遼		
960–1279 CE	**Song** 宋	Northern Song 北宋	
		Southern Song 南宋	
1271–1368 CE	**Yuan** 元		
1368–1644 CE	**Ming** 明		
1644–1911 CE	**Qing** 清		

Reference Table 2:
Symbolic Meanings of the Heavenly Stems

Direction	East		South	
Spiritual animal	**Green Dragon**		**Red Bird**	
Heavenly Stem	甲 Jia	乙 Yi	丙 Bing	丁 Ding
Brief meaning	Initiating Pushing Surging A sprout breaking through the earth	Flexibility with strength Early growth with bendable branches Moving around barriers	Expanding life force All things are clear and obvious	New life fully grown Everything is at its strongest
Number	First	Second	Third	Fourth
Element	Yang Wood	Yin Wood	Yang Fire	Yin Fire
Organ	GB	LV	SI	HT
Season	Spring		Summer	
Color	Green		Red	
Flavor	Sour		Bitter	
Fruit	Plum		Apricot	
System	Nervous system		Circulatory system	
Body layer	Nerves		Blood	

Center		West		North	
Yellow Phoenix		**White Tiger**		**Black Turtle Snake**	
戊 Wu	己 Ji	庚 Geng	辛 Xin	壬 Ren	癸 Gui
Blooming Flourishing Luxuriant growth	Distinguish-able features develop Things start to become hidden inside	Fullness Ripeness Beginning of reversal	Withdrawal Harvest	Yang energy begins again inside/under earth/water	Re-gathering the life force Everything can be estimated
Fifth	Sixth	Seventh	Eighth	Ninth	Tenth
Yang Earth	Yin Earth	Yang Metal	Yin Metal	Yang Water	Yin Water
ST	SP	LI	LU	BL	KD
Four seasons (harmonizing)		Autumn		Winter	
Yellow/brown		White/golden		Black/blue	
Sweet		Spicy/pungent		Salty	
Date		Peach		Chestnut	
Digestive system		Respiratory system		Genitourinary system	
Muscles		Skin		Bones	

Reference Table 3:
Symbolic Meanings of the Earthly Branches

Direction	North		East		
Earthly Branch	子 Zi	丑 Chou	寅 Yin	卯 Mao	辰 Chen
Hidden Stems	癸	己辛癸	甲戊丙	乙	戊癸乙
Brief meaning	Yang hidden in Yin A sprout about to grow	Intertwining energy Under-ground growth	Advancing moving forward A sprout stretching out of the ground	Flourish Surge	The time of full awakening
Number	First	Second	Third	Fourth	Fifth
Animal	Rat	Ox	Tiger	Rabbit	Dragon

South			West			North
巳 Si	午 Wu	未 Wei	申 Shen	酉 You	戌 Xu	亥 Hai
丙戊庚	丁己	乙丁己	戊庚壬	辛	丁戊辛	甲壬
Preparing for full ripeness	Against or reverse Growth at its peak	Fully ripe Uncertain Not yet decided	Stretch Expand	Extend	Retreat from the visible	A seed awaiting the next growth cycle
Sixth	Seventh	Eighth	Ninth	Tenth	Eleventh	Twelfth
Snake	Horse	Goat	Monkey	Rooster	Dog	Pig

Reference Table 4:
TianGan DiZhi Internal Alchemy Practice

TianGan DiZhi	Facing direction	Visualization—Inhalation	Visualization—Exhalation
Jia 甲	East	Green Qi entering gallbladder	Gallbladder
Yi 乙	East	Green Qi entering liver	Liver
Bing 丙	South	Red Qi entering small intestine	Small intestine
Ding 丁	South	Red Qi entering heart	Heart
Wu 戊	Northeast	Yellow Qi entering stomach	Stomach
Ji 己	Southwest	Yellow Qi entering spleen and pancreas	Spleen
Geng 庚	West	White Qi entering large intestine	Large intestine
Xin 辛	West	White Qi entering lung	Lung
Ren 壬	North	Mystical Qi entering bladder	Bladder
Gui 癸	North	Mystical Qi entering kidney	Kidney
Zi 子	North	Mystical Qi entering kidney	Gallbladder meridian
Chou 丑	Northeast	Yellow Qi entering spleen and pancreas	Liver meridian
Yin 寅	Northeast	Green Qi entering gallbladder	Lung meridian
Mao 卯	East	Green Qi entering liver	Large intestine meridian
Chen 辰	Southeast	Yellow Qi entering stomach	Stomach meridian
Si 巳	Northeast	Red Qi entering small intestine	Spleen meridian
Wu 午	South	Red Qi entering heart	Heart meridian
Wei 未	Southwest	Yellow Qi entering spleen and pancreas	Small intestine meridian
Shen 申	Southwest	White Qi entering large intestine	Bladder meridian
You 酉	West	White Qi entering lung	Kidney meridian
Xü 戌	Northwest	Yellow Qi entering stomach	Pericardium meridian
Hai 亥	Northwest	Mystical Qi entering bladder	Triple burner meridian

Index